Edmonton

Stories from the River City

TONY CASHMAN

Edmonton

Stories from the River City

Edmonton

Stories from the River City

THE UNIVERSITY OF
ALBERTA PRESS

TONY CASHMAN

Published by
The University of Alberta Press
Ring House 2
Edmonton, Alberta   T6G 2E1

Copyright © 2002 Tony Cashman

NATIONAL LIBRARY OF CANADA CATALOGUING IN PUBLICATION DATA

Cashman, Tony, 1923–
    Edmonton

    ISBN 0-88864-392-6

    1. Edmonton (Alta.)--History--Anecdotes. 2. Edmonton (Alta.)--Biography. I. Title.
FC3696.36.C37 2002   971.23'34   C2002-910220-0   F1079.5.E3C37 2002

Printed and bound in Canada by Houghton-Boston, Saskatoon, Saskatchewan.
∞ Printed on acid-free paper.
Proofreading assistance by Tara Taylor.

The University of Alberta Press is committed to protecting our natural environment. As part of our
efforts, this book is printed on stock produced by New Leaf Paper: it contains 100% post-consumer
recycled fibres and is acid- and chlorine-free.

The University of Alberta Press acknowledges the financial support of the Government of Canada
through the Book Publishing Industry Development Program for its publishing activities. The Press also
gratefully acknowledges the support received for its program from the Canada Council for the Arts.

THE CANADA COUNCIL | LE CONSEIL DES ARTS
FOR THE ARTS | DU CANADA
SINCE 1957 | DEPUIS 1957

Canadä

The Lineup

Foreword

Tony Cashman has done it again.

Edmonton: Stories from the River City may be the best yet for Edmonton's chronicler of history made entertaining and accessible. Tony would credit his material: certainly Edmonton boasts as many colourful characters and daring deeds as any Canadian city. Indeed, a large part of the Cashman appeal is his style of understatement.

But surely no other Canadian city can point to such a collection of tales well told. Here are the world-famous: Cyrus Eaton selling the public of Edmonton and Strathcona on sourcing gas from surplus straw. Emily Carr painting Edmonton. Sir George Simpson organizing the first winter tour of Hawaii for Edmontonians. And who was the first Edmontonian to visit Honolulu? Here's a clue: it was in 1842!

Here, too, are the elements of our social, political and economic history: the railroads, theatres, bars, hotels, even the cigar factories of Edmonton and Strathcona (once known as "Edmonton South").

Tony devotes one of his best chapters to the saga of John Michaels, the newsboy from New York's lower east side who, through his world-famed Mike's News Stand and his Newsboys Band, confirmed Edmontonians' belief that theirs was a cosmopolitan world city.

Here, brought to life, among the mud and dust, the clamour of fire bells and the clanking of streetcars, are free trader John Norris, who bamboozled the mighty Hudson's Bay Company; Dick Rice, who turned a zany city loose on the radio; Bill Noak the butcher, whose end-of-week meat auctions kept many Depression-era families from malnutrition.

These tales are uniformly entertaining. They are historically accurate. They portray a public spirit unique to our frontier tradition, manifested in "passing the hat" for a new wooden sidewalk, in North America's most creative neon signage, and in the use of popular will and main force in thrusting our province and its capital to the forefront, as told in the title story.

I am honoured and pleased to have been asked to write this foreword. As Edmonton embarks on its third century, riding the crest of its greatest boom, this history, part of our soul, would have been lost, but for Tony.

Our families arrived here in the same year, 1906. Our lives have intertwined more than once: as a teenager, I became a devoted fan of Tony's "Edmonton Stories" on radio. He was my boss at CKUA in the late 1960s. He wrote the biography of my wife's grandfather, J.J. Bowlen. But our first relationship is uppermost in my mind: I delivered the *Journal* to Tony and Veva some fifty years ago to their upstairs suite in a house on 102 Avenue, just off 115 Street. His paperboy salutes him.

THE HONOURABLE JIM EDWARDS
Chair, Board of Governors
University of Alberta

1

Three

Cheers

for

Edmonton

"**T**hree cheers for Edmonton!" cried the man at the back of the hall.

The hall was Scott Robertson's, above his store on east Jasper Avenue.

The night was July 31, 1905.

The occasion was a town meeting.

The subject was the inauguration of the province.

In thirty-two days Alberta would become a province. Edmonton would be the capital, but there would be no public ceremonies. Saskatchewan was to be a province the same day. The governments of Canada and the Northwest Territories had decreed that one celebration would do for both and it would be in Regina — a parade, a concert, and a ball, for which Regina had been awarded funds. Regina had also been awarded the dignitaries. Governor General Earl Grey and Prime Minister Sir Wilfrid Laurier would be coming to Pile-o'-Bones, and the celebration would not even be on September first, actual birthdate of the new provinces. It would be on the following Monday, the fourth, Labour Day, when the annual march of the trade unions would guarantee numbers for a parade.

Indignation stirred the dust on Jasper Avenue. Should Edmonton go it alone and stage a more mammoth parade, a grander concert, a more glittering ball? Edmonton's first city council wanted to test public opinion on spending $8,000 on the big show and called the public meeting.

It had to be $8,000 because that was what Regina was getting from the federal and territorial governments. So how much was $8,000 in today's terms? If, as the newspapers and the boosters claimed, Edmonton had a population of 7,500, which it probably didn't, that would be about a dollar a head. With today's indisputable population that would be $650,000. But a dollar was worth more then, representing a typical day's wage. Today, a person working eight hours at minimum wage earns about forty dollars. Multiply by forty and the crowd in Robertson's Hall was cheering for $26 million.

At ten minutes to nine Mayor K.W. McKenzie declared the meeting open, telling the crowd of two hundred the inaugural was the occasion of a lifetime in which the city could not be small.

Former mayor William Short said it was not only the opportunity of a lifetime but many lifetimes, and moved that the meeting endorse the cost.

Future mayor John A. McDougall seconded the motion, saying Edmonton was the provisional capital only and should lose no opportunity to make it permanent. City council would do its duty, but if not the businessmen would put on the show.

A.T. Cushing agreed the show would be for business reasons and the good of the city rather than "a high old time."

Mr. Kirpie said he was present on behalf of the German citizens and they were heartily in favour.

Alderman Charlie May said Edmonton could not afford to act small or mean. We might get some of the cost back from the government but we must go ahead now.

The mayor then put Mr. Short's motion to the assembly, all in favour to signify by a show of hands. Wrote a witness: "A perfect fusillade of hands shot up."

Opposed? Not a hand appeared as eyes charged with booster spirit scanned the crowd for traitors. The silence of total unanimity got to the man in the back of the hall.

"Three cheers for Edmonton!" he cried.

As the last hurrah faded, the mayor and alderman trooped down the wooden stairs, came out along Jasper Avenue, turned the corner of the Alberta Hotel, crossed dusty 98 Street to the fire hall, climbed the stairs to the council chamber, convened a special meeting, voted to spend $8,000, and adjourned at 9:27 p.m.

Thirty-seven minutes had elapsed since the mayor's call to order in Robertson's Hall. And there was no time to waste. Only thirty-two days to go, actually one less because the jubilation was to begin the evening before.

II

The mayor's committee plunged ahead, planning a multi-faceted event. Old-timer James McDonald, who farmed outside the city in present-day Cromdale, was organizing the mammoth parade. Billy Lines, manager of the brewery, was lining up schools for the parade, with the idea that no kid would be a spectator — big ones would march, small ones would be on wagons pulled by Billy's big brewery horses. Lumberman W.H. Clark had $500 for bands, with a mandate to make the streets resound with brass and pipes for two full days. William Short, in charge of decorations, pledged to make Jasper Avenue vibrant with triumphant arches, red-white-and-blue bunting by day and electricity by night — and he had valuable help from J.I. Mills who'd created our first electric sign four years earlier. Merchant Joe Morris, who owned the first automobile in town, was arranging sporting events, including lacrosse, Canada's national game. C.W. Strathy, convener of the grand concert at the Thistle Rink on the eve of the great day, is something of a mystery, but Vernon Barford is not. He was rehearsing a choir which was demographically revealing — twenty-nine men to only eight ladies. Tom Turnbull, for ten years manager of the Bank of Commerce, was organizing the glittering ball at the Thistle, the climax of the celebration. John A. McDougall was in charge of accommodation for the important people Ottawa said wouldn't be coming. Mayor McKenzie had a special responsibility. He was in charge of inviting them.

III

On the evening of August 12, a telegraph boy pedalled furiously out to 106 Street to the home of Mayor McKenzie, bearing a telegram from Captain Hanbury Williams, aide to the Governor General.

He brought the best of all possible news. Feeling elation on behalf of all citizens the mayor read:

"It will give Their Excellencies much pleasure to be present in Edmonton on September 1st."

The mayor had cut through two levels of protocol, territorial and federal, with a direct invitation to the personal representative of King Edward VII, confounding the high and the mighty who had declined to send one nickel of their distinguished presences to Edmonton. Most improper of course, but Earl Grey was a sport. In his term he donated a silver trophy for which Canada's football teams still compete, including Edmonton's with marked results. With nineteen days to go, the response of Earl Grey gave a purely civic affair vice-regal stature.

IV

August 23rd ... eight days to go ... and Edmonton was up to its ears in good news.

The Prime Minister was coming to the big show.

A famous British author was coming as his guest.

The Mounted Police were coming — to stage a musical ride.

A lieutenant-governor had been appointed for Alberta — and he was coming.

And Radcliffe wasn't — that was special good news.

Cartoon by Yardley Jones;
used by permission.

The reluctant presence of Sir Wilfrid Laurier would guarantee silver-tongued oration to go with the bands and cannons.

His guest was British parliamentarian Sir Gilbert Parker, who wrote stirring historical novels like *Seats of the Mighty*. Sir Gilbert would certainly have something rousing to write about after attending our inaugural. Strange that he never did.

Inspector Knight was up from North-West Mounted Police headquarters in Regina to deliver his good news in person. A force of two hundred Mounties with their mounts was coming by special train. The very next day twenty cars pulled by two steam locomotives would leave Regina. The train would steam down Mill Creek on tracks of the Edmonton Yukon and Pacific Railway, and the scarlet riders would camp and perform on the Rossdale fair grounds.

To the office of lieutenant-governor George Hedley Vicars Bulyea, of Qu'Appelle, brought a portly figure made to order for the ceremonial cloak and ponderous plumed hat. He was well known and had been recently in town as commissioner of public works in the cabinet of the Northwest Territories.

The word on Radcliffe was a good-news bonus. Originally he'd been the only government dignitary scheduled to visit Edmonton. On the eve of the big day he was to officiate at the demise of Charlie King, convicted of murdering an English hunter who'd hired him as a guide. The committee had been pressing for a delay so Radcliffe's gloomy specialty would not mar the celebration. The hangman was put on hold.

With the sudden prospect of all those VIPs the committee went to the Alberta Hotel and booked ten rooms. They went across the street to the Queens and booked ten more. They went to Alberta College and booked twenty-five student rooms. They hired twenty-five rigs and printed VIP meal tickets, good at any café in town.

An obscure prairie town had shown Ottawa it couldn't fight city hall. Edmonton had overcome reluctance and downright resistance in the highest places to ensure that the capital of Alberta would have a proper celebration on the proper date. And all in a month. If that could happen, what couldn't?

As the man in the back of the hall put it: Three cheers for Edmonton!

2

Emily
Carr
Paints
Edmonton

In July 1910 the boosters of Edmonton would have been nervous if they had known that Emily Carr was heading this way. The artist was on the train, on the first stage of a journey from Victoria to Paris, and was to break the trip at Edmonton to leave her dog with a friend. Although her art had not yet developed the strong line and hammering colour that made her famous, her prose had. On the night of July 16, 1910 she was in Banff and our boosters would have trembled if they had known what she was writing in her chronicle about the jewel of the Canadian Rockies.

"Banff is a beastly place, heat intense and mosquitoes worse than [Lake] Louise. The hotel is crowded and the food poor while the rates are very high. We meet two painfully energetic Victorian [women] who have derived great benefit from the sulphur baths and are indefatigable in dragging us, glorified by halos of mosquitoes, to see sulphur, smell

Edmonton as seen by Emily Carr.
Image courtesy of the Provincial Archives of British Columbia; used by permission.

sulphur, and drink sulphur. I am convinced that sulphur and all per-taining to it savours of the devil."

Having put Banff in its place, Emily Carr travelled a day closer to Edmonton and demolished the pretensions of Calgary to elegance or distinction.

"An unspeakably wretched day. Train crowded, dust flying, babes yelling, heat sweltering, bring us to Calgary about 4 p.m. Bramer Lodge, swathed in gentility and bathed in sultry heat, is locked in a holy sab-bath calm. The manageress, with small knob of hair resembling an onion, sits at her desk with a dog to the right, dog to the left, studying a book of sermons which she grudgingly leaves to attend to our accom-modation."

While Edmontonians would have been delighted by this impression of Calgary, on the morning of July 18 they'd have been something less than delighted if they'd known that the critic was on board a train steaming north, in company with her sister Alice, and Billie, the woolly mutt who was to be boarded here while the artist studied in Paris. But they didn't know she was coming because they'd never heard of Emily Carr, nor had anyone else beyond the snug world of Victoria and Vancouver. Her first day in Edmonton moved her to write:

"A heavy thunderstorm and deluges of rain. Sister and I [make] a little expedition having a taste of the Edmonton mud, a glutinous substance of a slimy, sticky, slippery nature. Before going a block your boots become so enlarged they are the size of a town lot, each one too heavy to lift, and you are obliged to stop and clean them with sticks before you can proceed."

If the local boosters had known, they would have been highly annoyed with her, as they were with Rupert Brooke. The English poet who wrote "some corner of a foreign field that is forever England" also wrote "Edmonton is a pleasant little town." A pleasant little town — what an insult! But they didn't read what Emily Carr thought about their mud because her chronicle was circulated privately among friends and the boosters had never heard of her in the first place.

In her fortieth year she was still seeking her identity. She thought she might find it in Paris, when all the time it was in the rain forests of her own Vancouver Island and the Indian villages of the Queen Charlottes. She had painted totem poles — at Skidegate in 1908 — but in the soft violet tones of Victorian flower arrangements.

After fourteen months in France she returned to reclaim the woolly mutt. By then it was December 1911 and winter had eased the problem of muddy streets. On this occasion she recorded an impression in paint rather than words and the picture is unique among her known works. A few show distant snow-capped mountains, but this is her only snow scene. The muted water colours are light-years from the relentless oils of her final characteristic style, but the boosters wouldn't have been any happier with the picture than the "mud" entry in the chronicle. At the moment of history immobilized by her brush, Mayor Armstrong was threatening to sic the police on the Dominion Census Commissioner for diminishing the true stature of the city. And Miss Carr appears to be siding with the hated census-takers. She is looking east from the back of what would be now 9929–103 Street. The Low Level Bridge joins Edmonton, population 24,882, to Strathcona, population 6,182. (There is no other bridge.) A lone pedestrian clumps down the steps from the end of 102 Street. A solitary dray has McDougall Hill all to itself. Along the top, the high school is a splash of red brick in a wood-frame skyline and the school is arrested on the verge of collapse, foundation sinking into a coalmine in the hillside. That "gopher hole" mine is an enterprise of Donald Ross, our first hotel-keeper, one of the greatest boosters of them all. Below the houses on the right he'll be greeting guests of the Edmonton Hotel, no longer the leading hostelry but forever number one, assuring them that Edmonton is bigger than it looks.

3

Sold

to the

Sheriff

Jack Rae held the office of sheriff from 1918 to 1937 and held it like a fortress, that is, in the tradition of his native Scotland, a tradition expressed succinctly by one of his predecessors, Scott Robertson. One day a young lawyer new to Edmonton and its ways called on Sheriff Robertson to introduce himself as representative of the attorney general of Alberta.

"You get the hell out!" said the sheriff.

The newcomer was Sem Field, who practised law in Edmonton for fifty years, left behind him the firm of Field and Field with fifty lawyers, and loved to tell the story of his reception in the sheriff's office.

It was Scott Robertson's way of informing him that in the evolution of British common law the sheriff had been delegated wide discretion in how the law should be upheld in any given case, and it would be unthinkable to have his independence of action compromised in any way by outside pressure, however well intended. Or to put it another way: "You get the hell out!"

Sheriffs in wild-west melodramas drew their independence from the same tradition, and the Wyatt Earps had other things in common with Jack Rae. Most were soft-spoken, and Jack was soft-spoken except when someone made him mad. Wild-west sheriffs were quick on the draw, and Jack was a great hand on the draw. Few could beat him when it came to drawing into the house behind an opponent's shot rock. The players in the lives of wild-west sheriffs were clearly labelled good guys or bad guys. In Jack Rae's office good guys were members of the public confused about the operation of the justice system and underdogs in general. Bad guys were pushy lawyers, creditors with court orders, and messengers from the attorney general. Jack might well have had Scott Robertson's greeting framed as a motto and hung in his office in the old Court House.

Jack's lengthy résumé contained almost everything but legal training. Born in Greenock, Scotland in 1870, he left for the new world at age sixteen and took sixteen more years to reach Edmonton. He was a draftsman with a lumber company in Toronto. Teacher in Regina. Teamster on the Calgary–Edmonton railroad project. Construction worker in the Kootenays. Gold prospector. Builder of riverboats for inland rivers of B.C. Sailor on a clipper ship plying between Vancouver and San Francisco. Carpenter in Calgary and member of Cappy Smart's volunteer fire brigade.

In 1902 he made his last move — to Edmonton — where he built houses and joined the curling club, the congregation of First Presbyterian Church, and the Liberal party. And that was canny. When the party formed the first government of Alberta, it had the appointing of people to the new civil service. Jack was made a licence inspector and went around the province upholding the law as it applied to closing hours of saloons. Saloons were open from six a.m. to eleven p.m., which seems generous enough, but there were always people who thought they should be open longer and made Jack offers to look the other way.

Jack said no to all of that, but he didn't say no when the Edmonton Professional Baseball Club came selling shares in 1908. He was issued share number one. Baseball was an acquired taste for a Scot, but curling came naturally and he was in at the formation of the Alberta Curling

Association and the Royal Curling Club and brought home many bon-spiel trophies. They were called challenge trophies — most were put up by breweries — and it was a challenge just to lift one, let alone find a place for it in the home of a winner. When Jack was past sixty, he took a rink down to Vegreville and arrived home with more king-size hardware — much to the delight of Mrs. Rae, of course.

Jack was appointed assistant sheriff in 1913, sheriff five years later, and his innate sportsmanship influenced his conduct of the office, most particularly in that troubled time of economic and spiritual depression when a sheriff's melancholy duty involved seizing the possessions of people in debt.

The sporting instinct led to one of Jack's finest hours. In one melancholy action he developed a strong liking for the unfortunate debtor whose furniture had been seized — balanced by an equal and opposite dislike for the creditor. As sheriff, he had to appoint a time for the goods to be sold at auction. The time came. Jack's pal the auctioneer called for bids.

"Ten dollars!" bawled Sheriff Rae.

"SOLD!" cried the auctioneer — and the dispossessed owner took his furniture home again.

There was a predictable ruckus about this, but no one — no one — told Jack Rae how to run the sheriff's office.

4

On the Air

When Dick Rice put Edmonton's first television station on the air in October 1954, he faced a demanding audience. The attitude was expectant: "Make it good! I've got hundreds of dollars invested in this box!"

But when Dick Rice put Edmonton's first radio station on the air — in August 1922 — the attitude was much simpler: "Make it! Please make it!"

In 1922 broadcaster and audience were partners in a great adventure. Listeners might have two dollars invested in a crystal set. They were ready to applaud any man-made sound running the gamut of static in their headphones. And it's entirely possible that more people saw than heard CJCA's first attempt at broadcasting.

Transmitter towers were on the roof of the *Journal* building, the studio in a fourth-storey room. The staff was made up of two. Dick Rice, the manager, was a wounded veteran of the Royal Navy mine-sweeping service. While visiting friends in Edmonton on a cross-Canada holiday he'd answered an ad in the *Edmonton Journal* for an engineer to operate the *Journal*'s pioneer broadcasting station. Dick's assistant, Frank Hollingworth, would spend some forty years with CJCA.

It was decided that Edmonton's (and Alberta's) first radio station should take to the air with invocations from the mayor, the ministry, and the chamber of commerce. The blessings of state, church, and business seemed to cover just about everything. Mayor Duggan was given twenty minutes to present the city's case, Canon Clough was allowed fifteen minutes for the clergy, and John Blue, secretary of the chamber of commerce, ten minutes for the business community.

The proprietors of the *Journal*, holders of the licence, were excited about the new medium but apprehensive too. In print, indiscretions and statements likely to bring legal action could be controlled by editing. But radio was immediate and spontaneous. To guard the *Journal* against indiscretions and lawyers, it was decided that everything should be written.

But there was a difficulty about this. To be heard, the speaker had to stick his head into a bell, something like the horn through which the Victor dog heard his master's voice. When the speaker stuck his head in the bell, he couldn't see his script. Heads popped in and out like ping-pong balls.

Mayor Duggan and Canon Clough soldiered through the exercise. Then came John Blue's turn. He started out bravely but popping his head in and out of the bell soon reduced him to confusion. Turning to Dick Rice he exploded: "Dick, I can't see a goddam thing."

It's improbable that any scandal was given. Canon Clough never met anyone who actually heard the broadcast.

Dick Rice experienced an even greater shock than John Blue's outburst while trying to open a window. High-voltage wires ran across the studio window. To open or close it, the operator had to put the station off the air. On the shocking night Dick tried to manoeuvre the window while the show went on — and was knocked unconscious.

Listeners at their crystal sets would not have complained about the station being off the air for two minutes. In the beginning, CJCA used to be off twenty-two hours a day, but might come on at any time for a special event, as when the vaudeville show finished at the Pantages Theatre (later the Strand) and Edgar Williams brought the pit band up to serenade crystal-setters with Barney Google and "Yes We Have No Bananas."

Harry Courtney played drums in the vaudeville pit band, Norman Clarke was on clarinet, Miss Matty Scaler played the piano, and Edgar

Williams the violin. Edgar spent many years in New York, but when Dick Rice put TV on the air he was back teaching and playing with the Edmonton Symphony Orchestra.

There was so much unused time on 580 kilocycles that CJCA soon had company. The frequency became a time-share, with the International Federation of Bible Students broadcasting from the home of their president, Frank Hobson, who was also chief boiler inspector for the province. Programs were originated in the basement of Frank's house at 9033–89 Street, transmitted from a pole on a farm in present-day Idylwylde.

Tom Crowe used to work in the transmitter shack. One night — it was, as the saying goes, a dark and stormy night — Tom was tuning up the tower while Frank and his pals rehearsed in Frank's basement. The phone rang. Tom was told that the transmitter was marked for a dynamite plot.

He called Frank. Frank and four friends jumped into Frank's car and sped towards Idylwylde through a driving rain.

Meanwhile, back at the farm, an explosion shook the flimsy walls of the transmitter shack. Tom streaked out the door, tripped on a guywire which sent him sprawling ingloriously in the mud, regained his feet, and continued streaking toward Whyte Avenue, which he reached just as Frank arrived. "Don't come any closer," he shouted. "You'll get blown to hell!"

The Bible students weren't concerned about being blown to that particular place and pressed across the muddy field to investigate. A neighbourhood farmer heard the commotion and offered to help. He'd been a sapper in the recently concluded world war, and his training came surging back. Sapper-style, he threw himself on his stomach and crawled through the mud and rain toward the shack. He heard a ticking. The ticking came from a parcel set against a wall. He dunked the infernal machine in a bucket of water and carried it off in triumph to his house, where police found a clock — wired to four batteries — wired to four giant firecrackers, one of which had gone off. Tom Crowe could never see the humour of the thing, even though Frank Hobson would laugh so hard telling about it that he became incoherent.

There was soon another station on 580 kilocycles — CHMA, station of the Christian Missionary Alliance — broadcasting from Buelah Tabernacle.

And CHMA led to still another. Jim Taylor and Hugh Pearson had Radio Supply Company, trying to sell radios, and thought they might sell more if people had more to listen to. So they made a deal with the Alliance. They'd operate station CFTP — T for Taylor, P for Pearson — and the Tabernacle would get three free hours on Sunday.

CFTP broadcast from a room in the Royal George Hotel, on 101 Street where Edmonton Centre sits now. Programs were sent out to radioland along a pole thrust through the window, a pole which outlived the station by many years. The operator was young Ted Sacker. As years went on he headed firms with his name, such as Sacker Electronics and Sacker Scientific. But at CFTP he was in partnership with listeners, experimenting with entry-level technology. Partners like Fred Young of Garneau, who found he could boost a signal two ways by attaching his crystal set to the phone line: the connection gave Fred both a ground and an aerial. Such discoveries were traded eagerly wherever radio fans gathered.

Only once was there an overlap in the time-share. Frank Hobson's Bible students came scrambling in over CJCA, giving listeners a replay of the Tower of Babel.

Frank said he wasn't guilty. He'd checked the *Journal* for that date and CJCA wasn't scheduled to be on the air. He produced the paper to prove his innocence. Then somebody pointed out that the date was correct but that paper had come out in April. This was May.

5

A Tree
Grows in
Garneau

The oldest tree in Garneau leafs out green each spring over Parking Zone N at the University of Alberta. The oldest tree stands unevenly at the east end of the lot. Drivers pass it on 111 Street north of 90 Avenue, an uncoordinated tangle of old thick trunks and young thin branches, a complex twisted by all seasons since it was planted there in 1874 by the man who gave his name to the district.

The oldest tree is a Manitoba maple, *Acer negundo*, alias box elder, alias ash-leaved maple, considered something of a weed in arboreal circles where it has another name suggesting it is no legitimate member of the maple family. Whatever its status, the Manitoba maple is a prairie survivor with tenacious native roots and will regenerate lost limbs. Garneau's tree still leafs out after more than one hundred and twenty winters. The house he built, the first in the district, was behind it.

Some called him Laurent (his official name), some called him Lawrence, many Larry. It made no difference: Garneau answered cheerfully to all.

Lawrence Garneau, with Eleanor, and the fiddle that made nights merry.
Photo courtesy of the City of Edmonton Archives, EA-58-3; used by permission.

He considered himself a farmer and he was a farmer of sorts, but he was best known for his fiddle, a rousing fiddle plied at hundreds of frontier dances, a one-man band with a rhythm section in the great heavy boot which pounded hour after hour on any dance floor the age provided.

So important was the fiddle that it put Larry Garneau above the law — above the herd law anyway — which was shown when his cows wandered off the property, trespassed on a neighbour's farm, and wound up in a livery stable. An important dance was coming at Ross Hall — still standing on Whyte Avenue in Old Strathcona above the hardware store of Will Ross. Larry was told he'd have to pay the livery stable to get his cows back. He informed the community that his fiddle would stay in its case till the cows came home. Which they did, promptly and without charge.

The dancing fiddle represented one side of his nature, but there was another which came of his ancestry. Larry Garneau was born near Sault Ste. Marie about 1840; his father was a French-Canadian fur trader, his mother an Ojibway girl.

When Larry Garneau was nineteen, he and some young friends decided to try fur trading on their own and struck out for new territory, to the upper Missouri River, around present-day Sioux City, Iowa. They found adventure but the attitude of their Sioux customers didn't seem to promise profits or long life. So they turned their backs on the wide Missouri and drifted to Winnipeg. There Larry met two people who influenced the rest of his long life. One was Eleanor Thomas, a striking blonde from the Scottish settlement of Kildonan, whose grandparents were three Scots and an Indian. The other was Louis Riel.

He married Eleanor and his Metis sympathies brought him into the causes of Riel. He was caught up in the excitement of the Rebellion of 1870, and when it was put down, many of the insurgents drifted away west — Riel to Montana, Garneau up the Saskatchewan River to Edmonton in 1874.

Here he found working making charcoal. Fort Edmonton blacksmiths were English, imported especially by the Hudson's Bay Company. In the old country they'd used charcoal in their forges and sniffed at the coal of which Edmonton was so proud. Converting it to charcoal made a living for Larry Garneau.

With a living secured, he looked for a place to live. Having almost unlimited choice, he staked a claim south of the river, from 109 to 112 Street, from the riverbank down to the line known as University Avenue. There he and Eleanor built their house and planted the tree that still leafs out after more than a century of winters.

The tree grew and the founder of Garneau lent zest to the social life of the settlement with his tireless fiddle. Then in 1885 Louis Riel came back.

He was in Saskatchewan, fighting for land rights for the Metis. Though Garneau's land claim here was never questioned, he sympathized. He didn't take up arms with Riel, but his sense of injustice, plus his sense of humour, was so keen that one night he just couldn't resist taking up his gun.

From his house he looked across the river to the present-day Victoria Golf Course and the campfires of Indians laying siege to Fort Edmonton. Across to the Fort, where nervous settlers were taking refuge. He cracked rifle shots into the tense air, just to get things buzzing inside the fort.

His shots in the dark certainly got things buzzing. Larry thought it was a splendid joke, even as he spent some weeks in jail for it; and when he emerged, the tension had evaporated and people who didn't appreciate the joke in April could see the humour of it in summer. He and his fiddle were welcomed home and social life went on to the beat of his heavy boot.

Time smiled on Larry Garneau. The settlement grew. Political alignments of central Canada took hold in the west and he was welcomed into the Liberal Party — into its inner circles. In 1894 he was elected to the assembly of the Northwest Territories.

But in Regina, the territorial capital, came a rejection that turned his life permanently towards the Indian side of his nature. He was barred from taking his seat because of his association with Riel — twenty-four years before in Manitoba.

In 1901, when he was past sixty, he left Edmonton to join in the heroic failure of St. Paul de Metis, an attempt to recreate an ideal Metis community based on the age of the buffalo hunt, a project out of the dreambook of Louis Riel.

The age was too long past. The colony dissolved into the town of St. Paul. But Larry Garneau lived on there for twenty years more, leaving his name in an Edmonton neighbourhood. And a tree.

6

Jasper
House

Since 1882 the Hub Hotel has looked down on east Jasper Avenue, ever since Thomas Goodridge put it there as the Jasper House, the first brick building in Edmonton.

In the beginning it was at the hub of commerce and of transportation too. Each Monday morning the stagecoach left the front of the Jasper House for Calgary, promising passengers they would make connections with the transcontinental trains on the following Friday evening. Except for the weeks of the Riel Rebellion in 1885, when Edmonton lay besieged, the stages loaded at the Jasper House. And when the uprising was past, the first overnight stopping-place on the road to Calgary became Fort Ethier, built by defending soldiers just north of modern Wetaskiwin.

The Jasper House was at the hub of social life. Edmonton's frontier "convention centre" was Robertson's Hall, a second-storey gathering place diagonally across Jasper Avenue. An Edmonton public school preserves the name of the proprietor, Sheriff Scott Robertson.

While Thomas Goodridge was planning the hotel, Frank Oliver's *Bulletin* reported a gathering of immense significance to those who believed in Edmonton and its future. On December 27, 1881 there was a

The JASPER HOUSE sign has obviously been added by photographer C.W. Mathers.
Photo courtesy of Provincial Archives of Alberta; used by permission.

dance at Robertson's Hall. It lasted from eight o'clock till dawn, and dawn doesn't come early in December.

The *Bulletin* took civic pride in the appearance of the dancers. In many cases their clothes were obviously store-bought. There was even a "clawhammer coat" (a tailcoat) among the fifty-six dancers. But most satisfying, for present and future, was the number of ladies. Sixteen. "The largest number that's been gotten together at any affair of the kind in Edmonton within the memory of man."

Thomas Goodridge's hotel became a social centre too. Like most hostelries of the day, the Jasper House had a second-storey balcony. However, Mr. Goodridge built the door leading out to it before the balcony itself, and in doing so provided an inescapable opportunity for an Englishman to add to the folklore of frontier Edmonton.

The Englishman was a unique figure of western mythology, a chap who modelled his lifestyle on *The Charge of the Light Brigade*, rushing ever forward, looking neither to left of him nor right of him to observe that he was no longer in the safety of England, plunging headlong into misadventure but ever able to snatch a quotable quote from the jaws of debacle.

Such an Englishman took leave of the rigours of farming at Clover Bar to enjoy an evening of refreshment with his friends at the Jasper House. Refreshment flowed swiftly and in abundance. Feeling eventually the desirability of fresh air, he charged to the door leading to the unbuilt balcony and launched himself into space.

He may have been shaken but his aplomb was not. Dusting himself off on the wooden sidewalk twelve feet below he commented: "By Jove, Goodridge, you've got high steps in your hotel."

7

Traffic
Cops

Strollers on the west walk of the High Level Bridge used to wonder about a padlock in the wire-mesh fence. It was a lock of epic dimension, apparently capable of securing a jail cell, which indeed it was designed to do. Sergeant Jim Smith of the city police put it there around 1920 to control speeding on the traffic deck. Another padlock 660 feet farther on was the second measuring point of a speed trap.

The locks recognized significant change. Before the first world war, traffic around the city was controlled by Alec Decoteau, the famed French-Indian long-distance runner. Alec patrolled the streets on horseback, arbitrating disputes between drivers of horse-drawn wagons and drivers of automobiles. Provincial law gave horse-drawn vehicles the right-of-way. Alec went off to war with the 202nd Sportmen's Battalion — along with sports like Wop May — and was one of those who did not return.

When the war ended, the city acknowledged that horses could no longer keep up to traffic, and although nineteen blacksmith shops still operated in Edmonton, motorcycles were issued to Jim Smith and his crew: Jack Irvine, Chris Shaw, Harry Ward the erudite Englishman, and Harry Crawford.

Three men were needed to spring the High Level Bridge trap. When the bridge opened in 1913 the speed limit was three miles per hour, and John Michaels, the news dealer, was fined for going six in a rush to pick up his English newspapers at the south-side station. By the 1920s the limit was a more realistic ten miles per hour.

When the trap was on, the man at the first padlock waved as a car came alongside. That was a signal for the man at the second lock to fire up his stopwatch. If the car travelled the intervening eighth of a mile in forty-five seconds or more the driver was within the limit. But if he made it in less, a signal went to the third man, who leaped through the cables, blowing fiercely on his whistle and waving the offender to stop.

Harry Crawford was the third man. He had the most dangerous assignment and got all the abuse from the speeding public. As one frequent flier grumbled: "I can get by those first two guys but I can never get past that blank-blank Crawford."

Jim Smith's crew measured out speed traps at other points through the city. There were three on Jasper Avenue — at Alex Taylor School, at 106 Street, and at 119 Street. There was one on 102 Avenue. There was another out on the St. Albert Trail, which, unlike other streets, was paved, and tempted the man with a hot car. Smith and Co. needed cover, and Edmonton of the time offered lots of natural bush even on important streets. But there was a problem with these locations. Checkpoints were marked with yellow paint. Practical jokers could confuse the issue and did.

Jokers could not hinder law enforcement on the High Level Bridge. However, there were few speeders to catch. Kelly the Plumber gave a dramatic account of the state of traffic.

It was a late afternoon in drear November, in the year 1916. Kelly was northbound in his Model-T Ford, rousing the distinctive Model-T clatter in the echoing girders. Toward the far end he observed a car stopped in the southbound lane. A man stood beside the car, waving frantically.

Chugging closer, Kelly recognized the waver as Doc Nichols, the thriftiest man in town. Doc's saving ways extended to gas. Passing 99 Avenue he'd switch off the ignition and let gravity give him a free ride down 109 Street and part way over the bridge. Only this time, as he went to reinsert the key, it flew out of his grasp and now lay somewhere on the dark deck. So he and Kelly searched the wooden paving blocks — which gave a smart clop to horses' hooves. The key was a small target but eventually it was recovered. Doc resumed his journey south. Kelly the Plumber proceeded north.

Between five and six p.m. they had blocked both lanes for twenty minutes and not a single vehicle — horse- or motor-powered — had been delayed.

8

The
Great
Streetcar
Race

The great streetcar race happened a long time ago, so long ago it was the last time Sir Wilfrid Laurier won a federal election and the last time the Chicago Cubs won a world series. Which means October 1908.

The great race was not between two streetcars but between two railroads competing for business. The system that delivered a streetcar from factory to consumer fastest would win the contract to deliver all future cars. Although Edmonton and Strathcona had a demonstrable population of 23,000, the boosters predicted an early metropolis of a million, a promise of many happy returns on investment for stockholders of the winning railroad.

The city of Edmonton, as the editors of the *Journal* crowed with civic pride, had set out to create "the only streetcar line between Winnipeg and the coast and nearest to the north pole."

The contest began on the morning of Tuesday, October 13, in the nation's capital. At the factory of the Ottawa Car Company, one car was loaded aboard each competing train and the race was on.

A man who picked winners by analyzing jokes would have bet on Canadian Pacific. Jokes about the CPR were bitter but respectful: "The cook ran off with the hired man? Well, damn the CPR." Canadian Northern jokes, on the other hand, were tinged with derision. "Here comes the engineer's dog — the train will be along soon."

The CPR came to the contest with a tradition of racing against time. Its trains hurtled across the continent with silk from the Orient while Canadian Pacific ships waited in Montreal to rush the cargo on to fashion marts of Europe. Against this, Canadian Northern had developed a unique racing tradition of its own: running to keep ahead of the creditors.

The betting man would have to give home-stretch advantage to Canadian Northern, with a depot in downtown Edmonton. Before the High Level Bridge, Canadian Pacific came only to Strathcona and CP's entry would have to shuttle across river on the meandering track of the Edmonton Yukon & Pacific Railway — down Mill Creek Ravine, up Groat Ravine.

CN lost five hours at Sarnia when its car got stuck in a tunnel and another Canadian Northern joke seemed in the making, but on the eighth day the competitors steamed into Winnipeg with CN slightly in the lead.

But from there on the inevitable pattern of underachievement took control. On October 22, CP's car was observed passing through Swift Current, but CN's had dropped from the sight of man. It was out there on the system, if system was an appropriate term, but where, no one could guess.

CP's victory train rolled on. Late on Saturday, October 24, it steamed into the Strathcona yard, and on the night of October 30, the winner was vibrating as streetcars used to do, on the brink of its first public performance.

Charlie Taylor saw to it that it was a performance. Flamboyant brother of Alex Taylor, Charlie was superintendent of the power plant

Car Number 13 is at the end of the line — perhaps of 95 Street and 110 Avenue. Watch that empty space. The city is coming fast. Photo couresy of the author.

and logically took on the street railway as well. He directed the necessary expansion of the power house and the laying of track — from 118 Avenue and 95 Street, south on 95 to 106 Avenue, west to 97 Street, south to Jasper, west to 121 Street; and inter-urban route to Strathcona — via 109 Street, 97 Avenue, Low Level Bridge and Scona Hill to Whyte Avenue.

Charlie and his gangs worked furiously — in two senses of the term — to mount the winning car on wheels and install the motors and trolley poles. Proud citizens who came to watch the work — in the car barns near Gazebo Park — were treated to sulphurous character studies of the manufacturer who shipped parts that wouldn't fit. However, Charlie had vowed that these proud people would ride the streetcar before the first of November. The gang hacked and sawed to make things fit, and the car was ready to roll on the night of Friday, October 30.

The *Journal* apparently had all available reporters out to cover the historic event. As they saw it:

Long before ten o'clock an expectant crowd gathered around the car and when the hour struck they were ready to clamber aboard. "Turn on the juice," requested Superintendent Taylor, and obedient to the command over the telephone, the man at the power house threw the switch. Ten minutes later with the crowd safely ensconced in their seats the car was speeding along Syndicate [95th].

...

Motorman W.G. Fortune was at the controls. Six years' experience in Toronto has eminently fitted him for the position of senior motorman in the city of Edmonton.

...

A few enthusiasts clung to the steps and rear of the car and a large brigade of small boys on bicycles raced behind, beside, and in front.

...

Chinatown en masse turned out along Namao to see the new devil wagon. Excited Orientals of the younger generation jabbered wildly and ran alongside the car.

...

The mascot of the car was a black and tan water dog which romped a few yards ahead and barked incessantly.

...

To the accompaniment of cheers by exuberant citizens the first streetcar rolled majestically into Jasper Avenue from Namao and commenced the triumphal progress along the main street until the opera house was reached [at 103 Street]. There further progress was barred by the tracks being filled with snow and sand.

...

The trolley was reversed. The car made several more round trips and the night was made lively by chases as citizens sought a chance to scramble aboard.

...

The theatre crowds were perhaps the most demonstrative. As the car passed them on their way home they cheered enthusiastically and in trying to produce as much noise as possible in return one of the passengers broke the bell rope.

...

"Oh, oh, he won't look. Make him look somebody, make him look quick." This was at the corner of Jasper and Namao. One of the young ladies had noticed a mere male on the curb and in her excitement to bring to his attention the fact that she was on the first car she nearly put her fist through the window. Luckily for the glass the young man consented to look up in time and the young lady caught a fleeting glimpse of him raising his hat and smiling as the car flew round the curve.

In the jubilation, no one paid attention to a freight train clanking into the yards of the Canadian Northern. But as the CPR's winner crossed and recrossed the CN line on 97 Street, the loser slunk into town. Canadian Northern had lost the race, the contract, and eventually its own identity in a pool of bankrupt railroads known as Canadian National.

But there's a twist, as there should be to any good story. Workmen in Ottawa had painted the cars, complete with numbers and logos reading Edmonton Radial Railway. The car loaded aboard Canadian Pacific bore the number two. Canadian Northern was given number one.

And although car number one missed the party, it now runs in Fort Edmonton Park, to give visitors a hint of the excitement that attended the Great Streetcar Race.

9

Milner's Hill

It was a freezing night in 1930 when Pop Lawrence discovered a piece of Edmonton's history. Pop was the man who introduced Edmonton to moving pictures — in 1908 at the Bijou Theatre. In 1930, when he was with the city water department, Pop and some of his pals decided the kids around 92 Street and 106 Avenue should have a skating rink. So one freezing night they connected a firehose to a hydrant and left it running, expecting to return in the morning and find a rink.

But by the light of dawn there was no rink, although the hose was still running merrily. A baffling puzzle. Then a distress call from Joe Milner gave the solution. Joe lived four blocks south, halfway down the hill, at 10245–92 Street. (The house is gone, but the ledge where it sat is still visible.)

A torrent of water was pouring out the entrance of Joe's abandoned, boarded-up coal mine and racing away with his precious hillside.

Pop and the boys had discovered where Joe's mine went when it disappeared into the hillside. There are still miles of tunnels under Edmonton's east end, from about 100 Street east. It's still possible to see where many started but not to know where they continue to — unless you happen to be flooding a rink.

They were known as gopher-hole mines, a method that started in the 1880s when enterprisers spotted seams of coal showing in the banks and burrowed in with picks and shovels, following the wanderings of the seam. Either Donald Ross or William Humberstone had the first — both claimed the honour — and one of Donald's gopher-holes undermined and ultimately collapsed Edmonton's first brick school, on the site of Alberta College. Fourteen known tunnels were dug under Grierson Hill, which is still on the move as a result. Excavation for the Convention Centre turned up several coal seams — and much excitement among onlookers.

In the nervous spring of 1885, when Edmonton lay besieged by the Riel Rebellion, our only set of law books was stashed in a gopher-hole mine — where 97 Street comes to the clifftop. And although the Rebellion lasted only weeks, it helped create and define a permanent rivalry between Edmonton and upstart Calgary, a product of the Canadian Pacific Railway. General Strange and the 65th Mount Royal Rifles rode the new rail line to Calgary and then pointed north to lift the siege of Edmonton. The kindly Calgarians told the General he was going to a very cold place. They didn't want him and his nice easterners to freeze in the dark. They urged to him take advantage of his last chance to buy coal. So he set off with fifteen wagonloads to rescue a town with nineteen operating coal mines.

Gopher-hole mines appeared along three cliff faces: Grierson Hill, Milner's Hill (east below Alex Taylor School), and further east still, the steep incline of Snake Hill. The slope below the Convention Centre was named for early enterpriser Del Grierson. Snake Hill was named for reasons now happily invalid. Milner's Hill was named for Joe Milner's father John, who gave up a position of secure prestige in his native Yorkshire to seek coal and wealth in Edmonton.

Back in the coal town of Bernsley, John Milner was cock o' the walk. The obvious meaning of the title was that he could lick any other miner in the house. It also meant that his fighting cocks were allowed to run loose on the streets of town, and that he didn't have to line up with other miners to get his pay. That was delivered to his home by the owner's personal secretary. But John Milner risked it all on the notion that he could

At the Mouth of a Coal Mine, Edmonton, Alta.

One of Edmonton's gopher-hole mines is celebrated on a postcard, in a set showing highlights of the capital. Image courtesy of the author.

do better in the new world. In 1895, when he was already middle-aged with a married son, his nose for coal led him to Edmonton and the slope that became known as Milner's Hill.

He bought twenty acres in Riverdale and formed a remarkable partnership with J.B. Little, the pioneer brickmaker. On Mondays, Milner and Little would work in Milner's mine. On Tuesdays, they'd work in the brickyard. On Wednesdays, they'd load Little's wagon and go about town delivering their products.

John Milner was so convinced about Edmonton he persuaded his son Joe to come out too, although Joe was already twenty-eight and had two young children. He arrived in 1902. He worked with his father for a time, then he went into business for himself, opening the promising coal seam that Pop Lawrence rediscovered trying to flood the skating rink.

Joe acquired the surface property around the entrance from that grand old Hudson's Bay man "Grandpa" MacDonald — official name

David — who had claimed River Lot 20 on his retirement from the fur trade and spent the rest of his long life selling it off piece by piece. Joe got the sloping land for a cow, a purebred Ayrshire that Grandpa admired. Joe was invited to pace off as much land as he thought the cow was worth. So he walked off so many paces up this way, and so many down that way, and so many some other way, and eventually so many back to the starting point — one cow's worth.

As the city grew, the Milners father and son each had a mine at Clover Bar and brought coal to market on the river. The overland route was time, temper, and profit consuming, demanding a dip through Fulton's Ravine, where friction could set the axles aflame — and at the end of the ordeal the coal was on the south bank. On the river, it could be delivered as desired.

In winter, coal came up the river on sleighs, in summer on a steamboat Joe had built, to the scoffing of riverbank loafers who said the thing would never work. It had a sidewheel, which they'd never seen, and the steam engine was mounted upright, something else they'd never seen. But it worked beautifully, its forty-foot length, twelve-foot beam, and draft of only eighteen inches slipping safely over all hazards, including Stove Rock. Stove Rock sat midstream near the present Beverly Bridge, usually just under water, and earned its name from an incident when it tipped a bargeload of settlers' effects and slid the kitchen range into deep water.

Joe could find hazards closer to home. One day he was coming out of the Baldwin Mine, another gopher-hole operation on Milner's Hill. Looking towards daylight he saw the way blocked by a black bear with two cubs. His only weapon was a miner's pick — and Yorkshire ingenuity. A coal car was on the miniature track at his side, a car that a man could push with one hand. Joe gave it a vigorous shove. The car emerged with a rush and roar, and the bears took off as Joe had planned. But he hadn't planned on what happened next. The coal car took off too, out over the tipple, down the hill crashing through trees, producing a runaway stampede of horses loading coal at the bottom.

In time, the small mines played out and natural gas squeezed the big ones. Joe Milner went into the regulatory side and became mining recorder for the Northwest Territories. Father John Milner lived on till

1925, attending social functions at McDougall Church in his turtleneck sweater and grimy miner's cap, which he regarded as a badge of office. His physical powers remained almost undiminished; as for his mental powers, in his final years he put over an undoubted fast one on the city.

City officials wanted some of John's property to build septic tanks. The site was up across Jasper Avenue, just west of Latta Ravine — some three-storey walkup apartments mark the site. John named a price, the city said all right, and property and money were transferred.

But John Milner had shrewdly and quietly, oh so quietly, withheld the mineral rights. He then announced that he was going to lease those rights to Jack Starkey, the flamboyant operator who already had the Penn Mine under the federal penitentiary. You can't build septic tanks over a coal mine. The city had to pay John Milner again. He was still cock o' the walk.

10

The

Honest

Safecracker

George P. Sanderson was long-living proof of the adage about the man who builds a better mousetrap. Right up to his departure from this life in 1939, at any hour of night or day, Edmonton's finest would beat a path to George's door, seeking help opening a balky safe — or a safe whose owner was balky about opening.

George said his talent was no secret; it was a gift, a special present from Santa Claus for being born on Christmas Day — which occurred in 1850 at Carleton Place, Ontario.

He was born into the century of "go west young man." By 1876, he'd gone as far west as Winnipeg. In 1877, he was further west, at Prince Albert. In 1881, he reached Edmonton, in the multiple role of blacksmith, gunsmith, and locksmith.

As blacksmith he was one of the first, if not the first, to use Edmonton coal for industrial purposes. Smiths of the Hudson's Bay Company, imported direct from the old country, imported their ways of doing things too. They wouldn't have coal in their forges — must have charcoal as in the old country. But George Sanderson said Edmonton coal could do the job, and it did.

His smithy was a fine building for frontier Edmonton — a two-storey affair of whip-sawed lumber, business downstairs, living quarters upstairs, located at Jasper and 97 Street, on the corner now claimed by Canada Place. There George and his partner Ed Looby shod oxen at twelve dollars per team and horses at ten.

A man of many talents, George had a dog with talent too. Snoozer, a sturdy, sharp-nosed dog of impenetrable ancestry, could drink beer and smoke a pipe — top-drawer diversion for a farm family waiting for a team to be shod. Snoozer was also a courier service. Edmonton had few houses. Write a message, put it in Snoozer's mouth, give him the name of the house, and he never missed. But Snoozer wasn't always on the job — thus accounting for his name.

In 1887, George Sanderson turned the blacksmithing over to his partner and concentrated on guns and locks. About the turn of the century he got out of guns and into safes — hundreds of safes, earning himself the title the Honest Safecracker.

On occasion, he was approached by gentlemen who'd made a study of a certain safe and were willing to share the contents fifty–fifty with someone who could open it after hours in the dark. With characteristic politeness, he declined, explaining that he was doing sufficiently well on legitimate business.

The formation of the province in 1905 gave his business a wider dimension. The country around Edmonton was opening up, forming itself into municipal districts. About the first thing a new M.D. did was order a safe in which to house municipal records — a huge safe, a gigantic safe, an iron monster which might keep the municipal council safe through an artillery barrage.

As one of the monsters was being wheeled into the M.D. office at Lougheed, it crashed through the floor and into the nether regions. George spent several days raising the sunken giant and repairing the mechanism.

On another M.D. occasion, he was called out at two a.m. to release a damsel in distress. The girl had locked herself in a brick-and-steel vault and the combination had jammed. The town police tried to come to the rescue with acetylene torches, but the steel door defeated them. So George made a thirty-mile dash into the night and in seven minutes had the lady out of her cage.

From his many trips into the country George came to know the map of Alberta as well as he knew the combination of the simplest safe. Among the tools he carried at all times was a Waghorn Railway Guide, invaluable to the man who must go to work since his work could not come to him. By mental calculation he could give the railroad mileage from any town in Alberta to any other.

He was happy in his work, with some exceptions, such as when the police called him on a case involving his friend Bill Buffy, who happened to be a renowned bootlegger of our 1916–23 prohibition era. The police surmised that Bill had a large stock of evidence in a big safe. But they couldn't convict Bill on that surmise, and he refused to be a sport and open up. With reluctance George did his duty, and in a couple of minutes looked in upon rows of gleaming bottles.

He was not happy to be called away from a family wedding party but couldn't refuse a messenger pleading for a patron of the Richelieu Hotel (later the Grand). A guest with a train to catch in ten minutes had some valuable papers in the hotel safe, and it was jammed. George trotted over and rejoined the family gathering as the relieved traveller boarded the train.

As George Sanderson worked on into his eighties, a member of the family party joined him in the work. Although his sight and touch were acute as ever, his hearing had dimmed and he couldn't be sure of hearing the tumblers fall. So his young grandson, Jack Gordon, went along to be the ears of honest safecracking.

George rarely showed artistic temperament, but there was such an occasion at Brule, the railroad town at the entrance to Jasper Park. He had been called to open a jammed government safe. It was a long job. A crowd watched — but from a distance. He insisted he had no secret, just a gift, but even the police weren't allowed to stand too close.

When the tumblers fell at last and the door of the safe swung ponderously open, he reached into a vest pocket and extracted a bottle. He was a temperate chap and a staunch member of a congregation which frowned totally on the distiller's art. But he believed that a man was entitled to drink to his success at the climax of a tough job.

But when the bottle hove in sight, the secretary-sheriff of the district began a furious tut-tutting. "Oh I'm sorry, Mr. Sanderson, we can't have liquor up here. This is railroad territory."

George Sanderson drew himself up to his full height of six-foot-two, which remained undiminished through all eighty-nine years of his life. Without a word he locked the safe again, spun the dial, and stalked out. Ignoring all pleas, he mounted a railroad speeder and headed off down the track to Edmonton. A week later he consented to go back — and charged double.

11

Hawaii
Calls

A winter getaway to Hawaii is popular in Edmonton. On a typical day there will be 158,000 visitors in Honolulu, several hundred from Edmonton. But it is not a new idea. Deep in the fur trade era, in the winter of 1841–42, the chief factor of Fort Edmonton spent a month there.

Jet planes deliver today's traveller to Hawaii in something like seven hours. John Rowand needed seven months. But it's unlikely that he could fly now, even if he was still around. Airlines have rules against carrying anything explosive, and that was John Rowand's outstanding trait.

He became the first Edmontonian to winter in Hawaii through his friend Sir George Simpson, supreme head of the Hudson's Bay Company, who invited him along on part of a journey around the world. In January 1841, Simpson was knighted by Queen Victoria and set out to see the globe, visiting all areas where the company had or might have business. Rowand the firebrand was Simpson's favourite fur trader. He enjoyed Rowand's "drollery and humour" and appreciated that "he had sufficient address to evade the truth when it suits his purpose." His sector of Simpson's empire (the Athabasca department with its capital in Fort Edmonton) looked eastward towards Hudson Bay and Britain. The Columbia department, including Oregon, Washington, and British Columbia, looked out on the Pacific, especially to Hawaii.

Although the gentleman adventurers claimed monopolies in North America, in Hawaii they competed head-on with traders of many nations, dealing products of the Pacific coast: timber, salmon, and flour.

In July, Simpson was in Edmonton and Rowand joined the tour, leading a trek through the Rocky Mountains to the Columbia River. The party left Edmonton on July 28. Even driven by tyrannical Rowand, who said a man wasn't sick unless he had been three days dead, they didn't reach the Columbia till August 20. On August 25 their canoes were at the headquarters of the department, Fort Vancouver, near Portland, Oregon. (Vancouver, B.C. did not yet exist.)

Then a funny thing happened on the way to Hawaii — actually, two things.

On September 1, Simpson set off to visit ports up the coast and in Alaska, aboard the Company's paddle steamer *Beaver*, a revolutionary novelty among sailing ships of the Pacific at 101 feet long and burning 10 cords of wood per day. That made Rowand the first Edmontonian to make an Alaska cruise.

Then Simpson turned south and Rowand became the first Edmontonian to spend a winter holiday in California.

Air travellers grumble at delays in airports, but Simpson and Rowand were held up fifteen days at the mouth of the Columbia River, as the Company's bark *Cowlitz* waited a favourable wind and tide to cross the bar.

Christmas was spent at sea, when beef, plum puddings, and "the choicest bottles" were broken out. On December 30, a helpful breeze carried them into the bay named San Francisco where the company named for Hudson Bay had a store.

Sailing down the coast, they called at Monterey, colonial capital of Spanish California. In Santa Barbara, they were entertained at a ball by Spanish society, and Rowand was a nimble dancer, notwithstanding his 300 pounds. On January 27, they left California and in four days picked up the trade winds and beat straight for Honolulu, where the Company had a retail store and lumberyard in present-day Chinatown.

Once a year, a supply ship brought goods from London. English mustard was a favourite, along with Cross and Blackwell preserves, ironware from Birmingham, Hudson's Bay blankets, valued for their warmth and softness, and coloured feathers for the topknots of Hawaiian ceremonial standards. Ships from the Columbia department called half a dozen times a year, bringing cedar shingles, 200,000 to 300,000 board feet of lumber, a third of the flour sold in Hawaii, and salmon packed in 180-pound kegs and pickled in brine. (In 1846, 1,530 kegs were shipped from Fort Victoria, with red sockeye the favourite.)

On the return voyage of three to four weeks, they carried away Hawaiian salt to pickle the salmon (fifteen pounds of salt to one hundred pounds of fish), molasses, and sugar. Sugar was the biggest employer in the islands, involving four hundred labourers at fifteen cents a day. Ships also left with Hawaiian sailors; the Company liked to hire islanders on three-year contracts.

On February 9, the snow peak of Mauna Loa floated on the horizon. To Simpson, some 110 miles away, it looked "like a solitary iceberg."

On February 12, the *Cowlitz* was being pulled through the narrow entrance of Honolulu harbour — as Simpson wrote — "by a crowd of natives who were elbowing each other on the reef up to their middles in water, all the while jabbering in their outlandish tongue, which, by reason of the numerical superiority of its vowels and the softness of the consonants, resembles rather a continuous howl than an articulate language."

Airliners deliver visitors to a city of 900,000. The *Cowlitz* brought John Rowand to a town of 9,000 — already developing character and tour-bus landmarks.

He certainly viewed it from Punchbowl Hill, where eleven heavy cannons commanded the harbour, establishing the military character of the Punchbowl. From its height Rowand looked down on Waikiki, playground of Hawaiian royalty, and on a town growing along streets with names like Fort, Hotel, and Beretania (Hawaiian for Britannia).

Simpson regretted that their visit was during "the dull season" when the King took the court to Lahaina to escape the winter rains. The upside was that he, Rowand, and their party of nine could rent rooms in the royal palace — a simple forerunner of the Iolani Palace.

Despite the social dullness, they saw much to interest the tourist.

"The grand recreation of the natives is the constant habit of swimming," wrote Simpson. "[They] are all but amphibious and seem to be as much at home in the water as on land; at all times of the day men, women and children are sporting about in the harbour, or even beyond the reef ...."

Away from the beaches, John Rowand's Honolulu held half a dozen buildings pointed out from today's tour buses. For greater convenience, today they're right on the route of The Bus — the ubiquitous vehicle of tourism — that shuttles visitors from downtown to Waikiki.

Beachbound along King Street, The Bus passes a grey bulk of church with a square clock tower, in the style of New England, source of Hawaii's Protestant missionaries. Kawaiahao Church is known as the Westminster Abbey of Honolulu. Volcanic isles offer little building stone, so native divers quarried the coral reef offshore, diving ten to twenty feet to chip off 14,000 coral slabs for the church. The roof came from a surprising source: the Hudson's Bay Company. On January 26, 1841, the *Cowlitz* offloaded 5 giant beams from the forests of the Pacific coast, each 83 feet long and 12 by 14 inches thick. These beams sustained the roof for 85 years and might still be if it weren't for a later import: the termite.

The company enjoyed superb community relations in Honolulu. When a rash British admiral forced King Kamehameha III to cede the islands to Britain, prompt and fierce intervention by Sir George Simpson brought the return of Hawaiian sovereignty. On July 31, 1843, the King attended a service of thanksgiving in Kawaiahao Church, and the Company gave its islander employees the day off and five dollars to celebrate with.

Past the church, tucked behind a row of trees, is the Adobe School, built in 1830 as a school and meeting house.

In the next block, The Bus passes two prominent landmarks of Rowand's Honolulu. The three-storey building of smooth coral, dating from 1831, was a storehouse for mission supplies. Next to it is the oldest frame house in the islands, prefabricated in Boston, brought around Cape Horn, and assembled on the site in 1821. The mission houses have been restored as a museum and historical information centre by the Hawaiian Mission Children's Society.

Inbound from Waikiki, The Bus runs on Beretania Street, past the mansion of the state governor, known to John Rowand as the home of John Dominis, wealthy merchant sea captain. Rowand was undoubtedly a guest there. The biggest house in Honolulu would have intrigued the man who built the Big House at Fort Edmonton, three storeys known as Rowand's Folly for touches like glass windows (the first in western Canada), imported from England in molasses to keep them intact. As monarch of all he surveyed from his Big House, Rowand would have been intrigued by the future of the Dominis place. It was to be the residence of Liliuokalani, last queen of Hawaii, who lived there till her death in 1917.

At Beretania and Fort Street, Our Lady of Peace Cathedral was half built, with divers bringing up more coral from the reef. What use Rowand may have made of the church, where Father Damien would be ordained for the Molokai leper society, is conjecture. Although Rowand was counted a member of the Roman church, he was noted more for punching out its detractors than participating in its rites.

Like most Hawaiian holidays, Rowand's ended because he had to get back to work. The Company ship *Vancouver* was loaded and ready to sail for the Columbia River. On March 1842, the first Edmontonian to visit Hawaii said *aloha*. With luck he'd be home in May.

12

Main Line
Fever

Through the month of November 1905, Edmonton was a hotbed of anticipation. Just settling down after the jubilance of September first, which launched Alberta the province and Edmonton the capital, the city was building to a celebration noisier yet.

The Canadian Northern Railway was approaching from the east. By the end of the month, Edmonton would be on the main line of a transcontinental railway — something to stick in the eye of a rival town two hundred miles south, which had aspired to be capital on grounds that it was on the main line of the CPR.

There was something about being on the main line. Stephen Leacock caught it in his *Sunshine Sketches* of the town of Mariposa, Ontario. Mariposans swelled with pride as the transcontinental train roared through, giving a glimpse into dining cars where gleaming tablecloths and cut glass were laid and smiling porters attended millionaires. The train didn't stop, but just being on the main line made Mariposa feel superior to towns that weren't.

Edmonton would not only be on the main line, it would also be an important stop for millionaires on their way to Vancouver. In November

A mass of brick topped with chateau roofs certifies that Edmonton is a main line city.
Photo courtesy of the City of Edmonton Archives EA 500-155; used by permission.

1905, Edmonton had main line fever, and the temperature rose with each bulletin on the advance of the builders.

No railroad could put down tracks like the Canadian Northern. Mackenzie and Mann, presiding geniuses of the line, held tracks to be the important thing. Builders of other railroads could rant and rave about roadbeds and ballasting and grades and curves, but tracks were what people wanted to see. And tracks were what paid off. Unlike the CPR, which dismissed local governments with feudal contempt, the CNR wooed them. Deals were made with subsidy and bonus clauses. Bonuses were paid on tracks, not roadbeds, ballasting, grades, or curves. William Mackenzie, the financial wizard, made the deals; Donald Mann put down the tracks. The builders were intent on reaching Edmonton on November 23. A bonus of $100,000 was at stake.

So much was on the line that Mackenzie, Mann, and their right-hand man W.J. Pace decided to share the wealth with the tracklayers. They were offered a bonus of ten dollars if they laid into Edmonton by the twenty-third. Ten dollars was a prize worth sweating for in 1905. Ten dollars would buy you a suit, twelve an overcoat.

One of Donald Mann's inventions sped them on their way. It was a gadget for putting down tracks, which the exercise was all about, and no other road had a gadget exactly like it. Mounted on a flatcar, it had two arms — one for each rail — to pick up tracks and slap them down. With fast-track building, Mackenzie and Mann cashed all the bonuses and managed to keep ahead of the sheriff until 1918, when the government merged all their achievements into the Canadian National system.

They were master showmen, extracting every ounce of drama from their business, making histrionics of history. On the morning of November 22, their gang was poised on the city limits — 111 Avenue and 84 Street. And that day they rested. The gang loafed — with ostentation and flair and casual banter with the curious crowds.

Then on the morning of the twenty-third, they erupted in a frenzy of progress. With the ferocious foreman aptly named Joe Work on their backs, Don Mann's monster at their heels, and visions of ten-dollar bills dancing in their heads, they raced along the grade towards city centre — across Syndicate Avenue (95 Street), Kinistino (96th), Namao (97th), Fraser (98th), Queens (99th), McDougall (100th) — while Edmonton extended the appreciation it offers to all championship teams.

They raced across First Street, past the new depot on the west side, going at such a clip they wouldn't slow down and stop for another three blocks.

The new lieutenant-governor of Alberta, G.H.V. Bulyea, in office but three months, pounded a vice-regal spike into the line. Then the track-layers formed up like a victorious army, and Mr. Bulyea and Mr. Pace moved through the ranks handing out ten-dollar bills.

The heroes could have bought new suits, but it's unlikely that many did. A celebration was afoot. Those privileged to attend all the euphoric events of that age said it was the mother of all parties.

A formal banquet was part of it. The grateful main-line city put on a dinner to honour Mackenzie and Mann, Pace and Work. It had to be in the biggest dining room in town, that of the Queens Hotel, on east Jasper where the Convention Centre sits now.

Then the whole gang moved across the street to join the crowd at the longest bar in town, that of the Alberta Hotel.

The din rose wave on wave. Bills showered down on the longest bar, floating in over heads of the crowd. One-dollar bills, two-dollar bills, five-dollar bills, ten-dollar bonus bills. Bartenders raced like tracklayers to keep glasses washed and filled. Whenever a man wished to drink the health of the Canadian Northern or Mackenzie or Mann or Pace or Work or Edmonton-the-main-line-city, he had only to reach.

The celebration of November twenty-third overflowed, literally and figuratively, far into the twenty-fourth.

13

Great

Expectations

1907

The city council of 1907 suffered from great expectations. Councils of that era, mayor included, were elected in December and served one year. The council of 1907 took office during the coldest, longest, hardest, meanest winter ever. But in tune with the optimism of that time, the population expected something great to follow.

Edmonton's population was reputed by its boosters to be twelve thousand, with so many arriving that one new booster in five was living in a tent. But they didn't mind the tents, being young and ready for the dance like the mayor, Billy Griesbach, at thirty our youngest mayor ever. Billy thought young — the previous year, as an alderman, he had been rebuked for carving his initials on his aldermanic desk — but as mayor he also thought big.

Rival Strathcona, half-concealed in the woods across the river, took out a city charter that year and celebrated its higher status by forbidding cows to wander at large. A wandering cow would be towed away to the nearest feed barn and would stay there till the owner paid the ever-increasing feed bill. The bylaw enhanced Strathcona's metropolitan appearance without costing any money — except to owners of stray cows — but Billy Griesbach and the council of Edmonton, urged on by the great expectations of twelve boosters, were going to spend one million dollars on improvements when the coldest, longest, hardest, meanest winter was over.

Potholes were not a problem because there was no pavement. Crusading Emily Murphy, who joined Edmonton's growing population that year, described the state of the streets. Jasper Avenue, she wrote, was "a morass of mud, a sweet-sour road over which horses strained and men swore in terms of uncompromising blasphemy."

Even mild-mannered W. Johnstone Walker was driven to stern language by the morass of mud. In 1901, sensing a westward trend to business, he decided to move his department store from about 98 Street to near 101st. In this century, a relocating merchant will merely move his business, but in Walker's day he could move the entire store. Most were like riverboats that plied the North Saskatchewan, wooded with flat bottoms. On the appointed day, draymen eased Johnstone Walker's store on to rollers and hauled it out onto the avenue. Then the rain came down. The rain kept up. The rain persisted. By and by, it rained some more. No amount of blasphemy could move the store. For a week it lay trapped in the morass of Jasper Avenue.

The city council of 1907 was elected to change all that — and more. It was authorized to spend a million dollars and borrow it on world markets. The men who undertook the assignment were all unpaid volunteers, even Mayor Billy, although at the end of his term he was voted an honorarium of twelve hundred dollars.

One councillor volunteered for extra duty as city health officer and was, poor chap, undone by his own zeal, which came about in connection with Norwood, that neighbourhood of dubious diversions. It was outside the city, across a weedy watercourse known as Rat Creek (now Norwood Boulevard), but when a report reached the health officer that measles had broken out among the ladies who entertained there, his sense of service transcended narrow corporate boundaries. Armed with a warrant of doubtful legal merit, he went forth to investigate. The ladies made him welcome, as did the bartenders and the "professors," probably including a piano player named Fred Studebaker who claimed "black sheep" status with the famed carriage-and-automobile family.

Eventually our hero recrossed Rat Creek, overflowing with good news (which was no news) about measles in Norwood, but then his public spirit became too much of a good thing. He began pounding on doors with his warrant, demanding to inspect housewives for measles — an angry delegation of whom descended on the next council meeting demanding his resignation, leaving council a man short in their difficult mission of borrowing and spending a million dollars.

As the meanest winter neared its stubborn end, forces in finance and nature combined to rain on our parade of progress. In April, the New York Stock Exchange went ker-rump. In May, the Chicago Grain Exchange went ker-rump. The Panic of 1907 was on. Edmonton couldn't borrow a million dollars in the United States. Our bonds had to be sold in London — with takers for only $600,000 worth, and at a discount of seven percent.

Some good things were achieved with this half-loaf. For $41,000 we got two fire halls and thirteen street alarm boxes, which were tested so often by the curious that the system was proved efficient without benefit of actual fires.

In June there was rejoicing over repatriation of the street railway charter. After an acrimonious struggle, the city got back the franchise it had granted Montreal capitalist W.G. Trethewey, along with his $10,000 deposit. But we couldn't borrow a further $49,000 to get on with track-laying, and great expectations were dashed.

Jasper Avenue was a bright spot. Some central blocks were paved, and of the transformation Emily Murphy was moved to write, "We are as proud of the pavement as if it were really chrysolite and jacinth."

The paving program, hindered by the economic climate, was further hampered by relentless rain, rain that made existing mud streets more vulnerable to damage. Iron-rimmed wagon wheels were slicing into them like circular saws, driving Mayor Billy and council to an emergency decree requiring wagons to run on rubber tires four inches wide.

Suffering most from rain delay were merchants along Namao Avenue (97 Street), second only to Jasper in mercantile significance. Namao had long been a muddy joke. Storekeepers put out planks so customers could cross to their side. They engaged in witty exchanges with teamsters whose wagons crunched planks into the mud. Wags put up signs in ponds: NO SHOOTING ALLOWED.

It had all been great sport, but the merchants were tired of jokes and through the mean winter came to expect great things of the million-dollar paving program. Namao was to have a storm sewer as well, and as the meanest frost reluctantly left the ground, ditches were dug. But the process went no further. Rain kept the ditches full so that pipes couldn't be laid, and pavement couldn't be laid until the pipes were in. The season passed and, adding insult to injury, paving crews worked on rival McDougall Avenue (100 Street).

At the close of the disappointing season, so many people wanted to complain to council that, in the interest of efficiency, Billy Griesbach hired the Opera House (at Jasper and 103 Street) so that all could complain in chorus. The section of the public that had what it expected didn't bother much about the meeting, but the disgruntled were out in force.

Mayor Billy sat impassive through abuse born of great expectations. And when the critics fell silent with exhaustion he spoke his calm, considered piece. He wasn't surprised, he said. It was exactly what he expected. The city could raise only half the money it hoped to raise. Therefore it could do only half the work it proposed to do. Therefore half the people were going to be mad.

Edmonton's youngest mayor then declared the meeting adjourned. This coolness under fire would serve him well some few years later when he became the youngest general in the Canadian Army.

14

Mike

Kelly

"The cars, the cars, the gol-darn cars, they're ruinin' the country and the police force too!"

That's what Mike Kelly said and that's the way he said it, and it was right that he should say everything three times because he was as good as three men if they threatened the peace of the community he was sworn to uphold from 1914 to 1950.

Mike was not a big man — his top weight was 180 pounds — but he had that square Irish build that enabled him to fire punches of equal power through an arc of 180 degrees. With his left arm he could throw a fist straight west and a moment later with his right arm throw a matching punch to the east. And being of average height, he could work in under a taller opponent.

Mike would take on three men without hesitation because his fine Irish discernment told him he was their match, and if an occasion required him to take on five men, or ten, his fine Irish temper would dispel any doubt of success. His reddish face would glow redder, his reddish hair would glow redder, and he would engage.

Ernie Peckover was a rookie policeman as Mike was nearing the end of his long service. On one of his first nights on patrol he was set upon by ten members of 96 Street café society. He managed to reach a call box and phone for help before they knocked him down. In minutes a police van whizzed up, and out jumped an old geezer with grey hair. Ernie groaned. What help would an old geezer be in a situation like this? But before he could pursue this gloomy line of speculation, the old geezer was throwing punches all over the place, three of Ernie's attackers were on the ground, and others who were able were disappearing with undignified speed. It was then that he realized his backup was the famous Inspector Kelly. As Mike put it: "Any man lays a hand on one o' my boys gets a seat full o' boots."

Mike spoke with the brogue of County Roscommon. Like many Irishmen, he began his career in police blue with the London Metropolitan force. Then he sailed for America with that wave of emigrants who won no empires for Ireland but won the cities of Boston, New York, and Chicago for the Irish.

Mike thought he'd try driving a streetcar in New York, but that lasted less than a day. A sarcastic instructor took him out on a car to show him how it was done. He made remarks about the Irish ... about Kelly's way of operating the car ... and about Kelly. Kelly stopped the car in mid block, and he and the instructor tripped the light fantastic on the sidewalks of New York with the instructor trying to stay in the lead.

Kelly drifted to Canada, to western Canada, to the police force in North Battleford, and in 1914 to Edmonton, where he settled for thirty-six years.

When Mike was night inspector at the downtown main station (98 Street and 102 Avenue), he began his shift with a walk up 96 Street and down 97th, to observe personally the night's prospects for riot, unlawful assembly, disturbance of the peace, and other events which make a policeman's lot not a happy one.

On 96 Street was a café called the Arrow, a grand place for all of the above. If the police were called to the Arrow three times in one night, Inspector Kelly would answer the third call himself. Younger men arriving on foot would find Kelly already there, throwing bodies out the door for them to catch.

Kelly had little patience with citizens who wasted police time. If he considered a complainant to be a crank, he might instruct a constable to go out on the streetcar. Or he might take a report form, tear a little squib off a corner, and say to the departing investigator, "There ye are ... there ye are ... gol-darn it, there ye are ... now write your report on this!"

Mike thought policemen should walk. A uniformed man on foot created respect for the law, and the man got a better feel for "what was goin' on." That's why he hated cars, the cars, the gol-darn cars. "The police ride around in cars and don't ever look at the back doors at all at all ..."

Mike also hated firemen. When he was inspector at the south-side station, he had to sit in his office and watch the firemen across the street playing catch — or, even worse, playing tennis — between alarms. He would growl a chain of unintelligible words from among which, every so often, would emerge the recognizable word *firemen*.

A devoted family man with five children, Mike also couldn't stand a man who beat his wife. One night he was called to a hotel where a professional wrestler, of fearsome build and reputation to match, was pounding on the lady he was supposed to cherish. "Ye stop it now ... ye stop it now ... gol-darn it, ye stop it now or I'll throw ye out o' here!" The wrestler gazed down on Kelly in disbelief, but met a glare of such fierce determination that he desisted and all was quiet on Mike's departure.

Kelly was ever willing to reveal an unexpected talent. One day, presiding at his desk on the south side, four telephone calls came in, each right on the heels of the other. Constable McCormack, hearing Mike's one-syllable replies, had no idea what the calls were about. Until the inspector leapt to his feet. "The dahgs, McCormack ... the dahgs, the gol-darn dahgs ... they're in the garden ... they're on the roof ... they're in the garbage ... the dahgs are everywhere. Git the dahgs, McCormack!"

McCormack tried but returned with no dahgs.

"A bone, McCormack ... a gol-darn bone ... git me a bone, McCormack, and a piece of gol-darn rope and I'll show ye how ye git dahgs!" Kelly soon had enough dahgs for a show, and in the garden and on the roof and in the garbage there were no dahgs at all at all.

One of Mike's finest hours came in the hungry thirties when he was on duty downtown. Word reached the main station of trouble brewing on the Market Square — just a block away on the site of today's Milner Library — more trouble than a dozen Arrow Cafés. Hundreds of unemployed were gathering for a march on the legislature. Conditions were ripe for smashing of windows along Jasper Avenue and overturning of streetcars. Kelly had seen enough of that in Ireland. It wasn't going to happen here, not on his shift anyway. He rounded up thirty constables and took a stand across the intended parade route by the McLeod Building. Kelly met the leader head on. He just talked.

And talked. And talked. The parade broke up — at the McLeod Building.

Kelly had another celebrated head-on confrontation. One morning he was driving to work down Scona Hill, driving the car as though he mistrusted the thing, which he probably did. Towards him, up the hill, came another car, slightly over the centre line on Kelly's side of the road. The other car kept coming. Kelly kept coming. There was a meeting of steel and glass, and doctors were taping up Mike's wounds. He could have avoided the collision by swerving to the right. But that would have been against his principles. Mike Kelly never got out of the road for any man.

15

Show
Business

When Edmonton was young and the towns around were younger, show people of Edmonton went out in troupes to entertain residents of the towns. This was the time from the early years of the twentieth century through the mid 1920s, from the time science made it possible for a man to farm in the Edmonton district to the time science invented the motion picture and radio-receiving set for his entertainment.

Show people of Edmonton presented their plays, sang their songs, performed their magic acts, and did their comedy routines in churches, community halls, and opera houses in towns along the railroad lines. The troupers who carried show business into the country were not all amateurs. Some even made a haphazard living at it, such as the presiding geniuses of Davis-Dalkin Productions: Eugene C. Davis, who became dramatic director for high schools of Cleveland, and Tommy Dalkin, who became director of technical services for the Alberta Department of Lands and Forests.

Right after the first world war, Davis and Dalkin went to New York to study dramatic production. In 1920 they returned to Edmonton and founded the Dalkin-Davis Academy of Dramatic Art. The academy was in the old Empire Block, and from the more capable students they organized a theatre troupe to tour the railroad towns, staging plays like *Smiling Through, Peg O' My Heart, Grumpy,* and *Waterloo.* They might go down the CNR line to Vermilion and work back home, or down the CPR line to Didsbury and work back home, being careful always to get closer to home, another trick Davis and Dalkin learned in New York.

Railroads offered the most reliable transportation. There was so little difference between main roads and side roads that motorists would get hopelessly lost, which the Davis-Dalkin company did one bitter winter night trying to drive home from a show in Leduc. Coming by happy chance on to the CPR line, they bumped the ties back to home.

They encountered other trials that illustrate the maxim that there is no business like show business. In the Lacombe Opera House one night, they were presenting *Smiling Through.* The big scene came where the jealous villain shoots the bride on her wedding day. When the villain fired, a six-year-old boy, leaning intently over the balcony railing, fell over the rail. He was retrieved by his father, who grabbed frantically and successfully at his disappearing trouser seat. The audience roared at this performance, ruining the one on stage.

In summertime, members of the company might make a temporary living in chautauqua, one of the great socio-educational movements of the time. Chautauqua organized companies of actors and musicians, and sent them on tent-show tours of pioneer towns thirsting for entertainment and culture.

Some talent was imported, but most companies were organized in the area. Elizabeth Sterling Hayes was engaged to direct the first play sent out from Edmonton, which went on a typical tour of the Peace River country.

Agents went ahead, setting up tents and organizing local committees to sell five-day packages. On Monday, the play was presented in a tent in High Prairie. On Tuesday, the play moved to a tent in McLennan while a concert entertained High Prairie. Wednesday found the play in Peace River, the concert in McLennan, and an illustrated travel lecture in High Prairie. And so on.

Young ladies of the troupes were a concern for chautauqua. They were attractive, obviously, or they wouldn't have been in the troupes, but the raw Peace River country was fraught with perils like swift rivers,

The cast of Dandy Dick *on stage at Holy Trinity Church — W. Bowden-Smart centre.*
Photo courtesy of Mrs. Harold Hawe.

deep forests, and commercial travellers. For protection against salesmen, guardians were engaged — the term *chaperone* was frowned upon — and they weren't older ladies embittered by experience, either. Chautauqua hired the ultimate puritans: kid sisters.

Reaching out to the towns originated with amateur troupes of the pre-war era, including the one from Holy Trinity Anglican Church. (Fittingly, the church has lately become a venue for the Fringe Festival.) A strong personality in this group was an accountant at the nearby Brackman-Ker mill, still standing under historic protection on Saskatchewan Drive. He was W. Bowden-Smart, an Englishman with a dash about him not usually associated with accountants, a dash lending credence to whispers that he had been on the stage in England and had left the old country "under a cloud." He never discussed the alleged cloud directly but probably encouraged the notion for its sinister effect.

W. Bowden-Smart starred in Holy Trinity's production of *Dandy Dick*. Dandy Dick, being a horse on a sporting English estate, did not actually appear on stage. W. Bowden-Smart played the lord of the manor, a tyrannical tease of a patriarch who annoyed his family by staying out all night and taunting their suspicions by chortling: "I shall punish you all by NOT telling you where I slept last night."

It was W. Bowden-Smart's big line, a hit in Edmonton and other towns, along with the play. The troupe thought it should be a hit in Leduc and boarded a southbound train.

It might well have been a hit if they hadn't decided to emulate the comedians who came through Edmonton on the big-time vaudeville circuits. Professional audiences on the Orpheum and Pantages circuits used to panic audiences with jokes about Leduc. The Holy Trinity crowd decided to be big-time too, and as they had dinner in their hotel before the show, made themselves merry with noisy jests about Leduc.

The townsfolk were not amused, and with about five exceptions, boycotted the performance of *Dandy Dick*. The snub, however, weighed but lightly on W. Bowden-Smart. In a personal tradition of show business, he was getting gloriously impaired. When the moment came for his big line, he fairly shouted: "I shall punish you all by NOT telling you where I slept last night."

Eventually the cast retired to bed in the hotel, but W. Bowden-Smart was not with them. He was treading the boards — of the wooden sidewalk outside. They heard him clumping heavily back and forth, declaiming. He was Hamlet, Macbeth, Othello, Iago, King Lear, Mark Antony burying Caesar, Ulysses on his final voyage, King Arthur expiring, Sydney Carton at the foot of the guillotine. Bits of Shakespeare floated up. Bits of Shaw. Bits of words. They heard a body slump against the building. They heard snoring, the rich, contented snoring of a man at peace with his art.

Morning came. The cast of *Dandy Dick* was in the dining room having breakfast. In walked W. Bowden-Smart. Dishevelled but undismayed, he drew himself to theatrical height and declared: "I shall punish you all by NOT telling you where I slept last night."

16

Jack Norris,
Free Trader

Jack Norris liked to tell the story of two brave men. Jack had a load of tales and he told them well, in the soft brogue of Scotland's western isles.

He told about running away to sea at age twelve. At age twenty signing with the Hudson's Bay Company for the Canadian prairies. Of working at Fort Edmonton in the 1850s — then going out into business for himself. In Jack Norris' day, the term *free trader* meant a man who dared conduct business in lands claimed by the Hudson's Bay Company. When the gentleman adventurers ran up the Company flag in territory awarded them by King Charles II, most men would salute. But there were pesky exceptions like Jack Norris.

The Company's Fort Edmonton stood on the site of the present-day Alberta legislature. Jack and his partner Ed Carey opened a competing free-trade store within sight of the Fort, a few hundred yards up the slope, at about 111 Street and 99 Avenue.

There Jack traded so shrewdly that in 1897 he was able to sell out his share of the business for a whopping $50,000 and retire to a farm — along the St. Albert Trail at 118 Avenue, where he was happily spinning yarns when Fort Edmonton was demolished in 1915. Jack had to tell his stories. He couldn't write them because he'd never learned to read or write — like Senator Pat Burns and John Gainer, founder of the packing plant.

Jack had a favourite about putting one over on the Hudson's Bay Company. It had to do with fishnet twine, an important item in the fur trade. The Indians were mighty fishermen, and the names they gave to many places suggested the country was jumping with mighty fish. Namao meant big fish. Sturgeon River was also known as Big Fish River. Lake Wabamun meant Lake of the White Whale, presumably an even bigger fish. Little wonder that fishnet twine was a major item. Little wonder that Norris and Carey were perturbed when they ran out of it halfway through one winter.

Jack had to go grovelling to the Fort to see if the Hudson's Bay traders would let him have enough to keep going. Of course. They'd be delighted to let him have all he needed — at double the retail price. Harharhar!

Jack considered this a hard joke, but there was nothing he could do about it. He needed fishnet twine, even if he had to sell at a loss. But a Norris of the western isles will find a way to come out on top, especially one who's run away to sea at twelve. His Celtic cunning evolved a plan. When an Indian pal came in to trade, Jack would bundle up some skins native-style and send him over to the Fort to trade for fishnet twine — and bring it back. A few weeks of this strategy and Jack cornered the entire fishnet twine supply of Fort Edmonton. Harharhar! A delegation of Hudson's Bay men came under a flag of truce to ask Jack if they might buy enough to see them through the winter. Jack said he'd be delighted. They could have all they needed — at four times the retail price. Though Jack was soft-spoken, he was never quiet, and he trumpeted his last laugh over the district.

Jack also told the story of the last laugh he had on the Mounted Police. Mounties appeared on the prairies in the 1870s, to maintain the right and uphold the law on prohibition of spirituous liquors. Jack had nothing against maintaining the right, but he considered prohibition a poor sort of law, not worthy of notice. On his wagon trips to Winnipeg for supplies, he would bring home a barrel of whisky, maybe two.

On the trip he told about, he was nearing the end of the long, long trail home, remembering the first time he'd seen the valley at Edmonton, when he realized it was the place he'd been seeking in his travels, the place he would settle. His mellow mood was broken by a sight beloved of artists: on a hilltop waited a scarlet-coated horseman silhouetted against the big clear sky. Jack knew what the Mounties had come expecting to find, and admitted he had it when they rode down to meet him.

As the Norris pack train ambled towards the setting sun, his nimble brain was dancing. They passed a swampy lake, weedy at the edges, which smelled as bad as it looked. Jack announced they would camp here for the night. The Mounties protested, but Jack insisted the horses were tired. When the sun went down, clouds of mosquitoes rose from the steamy grass.

The police withdrew to high ground, taking Jack for safekeeping, leaving his head man in charge of horses and freight. Under shelter of night, the head man did what Jack figured he'd do. When he was brought into court, the only evidence against him was two barrels of revolting slough water.

Jack got a lot of practice telling that one, but his favourite was the story of two brave men. It happened back in the olden days, before the Mounties came to prohibit liquor, when rum was a staple of the fur trade, when Jack was still an employee of the Hudson's Bay Company. One brave man was himself, the other a large and well-muscled Indian customer of Fort Edmonton.

It was a summer evening. Jack was out west of the Fort, bringing up kegs of rum. The Indian sidled up. He spoke.

"Jack?"

"Yeah?"

"Look at the scenery, Jack."

"It's lovely scenery, all right."

"Look at the sunset."

"It's a lovely sunset, all right."

"Take a GOOD look at the sunset."

"Why should I take a GOOD look at the sunset?"

"Because you'll never see it again."

"Oh, why won't I ever see it again?"

"Because you spit in my face today, Jack, and I'm gonna KILL you."

"That's just what I'm gonna do to YOU!" Jack exploded.

He jumped to face his assassin, in the same motion uncorking a wild roundhouse right. At the same moment, the assassin uncorked a wild roundhouse right. Both missed. Jack swung with such abandon that he pulled himself right off his feet and landed face down in the grass. Picking himself up, he didn't look for a fight. He saw the protecting walls of the Fort and streaked for safety. Nearing the gate, he glanced back to see if his pursuer was gaining. Far away he saw the Indian disappearing over the prairies as fast as moccasins would carry him.

The Story of Two Brave Men. Jack Norris would have the last laugh, even if it was on himself.

17

Didn't You
Used to Be...?

It's not unusual for a man to have been something else in his career, but Fred Marshall stretched it to the limit. Fred used to be the Dawson Bridge. In the summers of 1909, '10, and '11, he provided the service since offered by the bridge.

Fred was an unlikely prospect for this position. In his native Somerset, England, he was growing up sickly with tuberculosis. In 1909, his parents heeded doctors' advice and moved Fred and the family to the clear air of Edmonton, taking a house in Riverdale.

Doctors had recommended fresh air and exercise. For the exercise part, Fred's older brother Ned suggested rowing a boat in the nearby river. The idea had merit — except that Fred had never been in a rowboat, so the Marshalls devised a learning experience. They got a long rope, with the boat on one end and thirteen-year-old sister Norah on the other, walking the bank. After three weeks, Fred cast off the training line and turned exercise to profit, hiring out as ferryman at five cents a ride.

He plied a triangle. Starting a block above the present bridge, he'd row one block across and one block down with the current. Then he'd row two blocks upstream in the backwash under Forest Heights. Then

The Dawson Bridge in construction. Looking west, Alex Taylor School dominates the horizon.
Photo courtesy of the City of Edmonton Archives EA 10-2083; used by permission.

he'd strike out into the current again, one block across and one block back to the starting point.

One passenger translated into a nickel, but when the boat was loaded to its limit — and with no extra weight of life jackets — he could make a quarter. In an average month he took home seven or eight dollars, not bad for a sixteen-year-old when adults worked for a dollar a day.

And the river offered other opportunities for profit. Emily Murphy described the buzz of sawmills as the typical sound of Edmonton summer. As a sideline to ferry duty Fred used to catch poles and fence-posts, which he sold on shore. His biggest catch, one that almost got away, was a flagpole. Sixty feet long and five inches through at the base, the pole put up a battle before he brought it ashore and sold it for five dollars.

Not all flotsam was friendly. Birch logs floating under water would strike the ferry with a bumping and grinding that brought passengers comfort of neither body nor mind. A birch tree once caught Fred and ran off downriver with him.

Facing backwards contributed to the incident. He rowed into the branches of a hefty tree adrift with the broken stump dragging bottom. Fred's boat was gripped tight in the branches. He was bounced along for two miles until he managed to nurse his arboreal kidnapper onto a gravel bar and make his escape.

From such adventures Fred Marshall got to know his river as well as Huckleberry Finn knew his. He could row the triangles with his eyes shut, navigating by changes of direction and force in the current. One night when fog hung so thick he could not see either bank, he made a successful crossing with a full load of coal miners. Coal men accounted for a good deal of Fred's trade. They would come across for an evening in town, and then along in the early hours of the next morning would be tapping on his window.

The militia was good for business too. A rifle range marked the site of the present Riverside Golf Course, and on Saturdays there were always citizen-soldiers wanting to hone their skill on the range. Fred had his biggest day through the militia. One Saturday he ferried 193 soldiers to a provincial rifle competition, running up a tab of $19.30. And through that experience he was introduced to the frustrations of bureaucracy. Colonel Cox, commander of the competition, assured Fred that Ottawa would be good for the bill. And Ottawa paid as the colonel promised — exactly one year later.

The river supplied fish for the Marshalls' table. Fred caught goldeye and ling cod, and once hooked a five-pound trout. His father Reuben once caught a sturgeon. But his biggest catch was a steamboat. He'd set a night line out into the river, a long line with half a dozen hooks weighted at the far end by a chunk of iron. John Walter's steamer *Strathcona* came thrashing past. The night line wrapped itself around the paddlewheel with the iron weight swinging free. Every time the wheel turned, the iron swung over and hit the wooden cabin a mighty smite. But the crew didn't notice. And Reuben and Fred watched their iron weight disappear around the bend, smashing the cabin to kindling.

Real estate promoters put an end to Fred's idyll. They kept relentless pressure on investors to buy lots in Forest Heights and subdivisions beyond, and on city council to build a conventional bridge to those parts. Inevitably construction began on the Dawson Bridge, but Fred Marshall still had a piece of the action. The lad who used to be the bridge spent the summer of 1912 as night watchman.

18

The Mail
Must Go
Through

Privatized postal service is thought to be a new idea, but it's not. That's how it was done in Old Strathcona.

George Thomson was postmaster. He was also registrar of vital statistics. He owned the Post Office Building — at 10364 Whyte Avenue, currently occupied by Carol's Sweets.

He owned the post office boxes — there must have been a hundred — and rented them for two dollars a year. He made a commission on money orders. He paid the staff, young lady clerks who worked behind heavy barred wickets capable of restraining a bear. And he paid the outside man, Tom McLean.

Tom was a tailor. Before and after each business day, he would go on tour of the street mailboxes of Strathcona, picking up letters. One small sack was enough to handle all outgoing mail. And Tom's contribution to the postal service enabled him to practise yet another sideline. Tom the tailor was in real estate.

Real estate figured in the mail: valuable building lots in swamps were promoted that way. But there was no mass-produced junk mail, no mountain of magazines, and, come December, no blizzard of Christmas cards.

Upon the swift completion of his appointed round, Tom would take his haul to the social centre of Old Strathcona. The postmaster was expected to provide a waiting room for the public. In winter, one of the postal services was a stove, for thawing country people who came to Whyte Avenue to shop. Around the stove country folk mingled with town folk waiting for it to happen: the arrival of the mail train.

It occurred each afternoon at about three o'clock. The train came from Calgary, and Strathcona was the final destination. The High Level Bridge did not yet span the river to carry trains into Edmonton.

Waiting for the train was theatre, a sort of advance echo of the Fringe Festival. Waiting for Godot doesn't hold a candle to Waiting for the Train. Tension built with talk of letters the train might be bringing, should be, better be, hadn't yesterday or all last week. Would the train arrive on time? Would it arrive at all?

By one o'clock watches were coming out. Checking time was not then a downward glance at a wrist. The wristwatch, like the cigarette, was considered unmanly. Withdrawing a watch from its pocket in the vest was a solemn procedure, second cousin to withdrawing life savings from a bank. When the watch was out of its hole and the cover clicked open, it was held out to the full length of the anchor chain securing it to the vest.

As the hands crept around towards the hour of three, odds against the train increased: one hundred to one against being on time, fifty to one against arriving that day. Five to one against arriving ever. Trains had been known to disappear off the face of the earth.

Then, just when you'd least expect it, at three o'clock, the train was clanging into the station, blowing clouds of triumphant steam. Hurrah hurrah! Some rushed to the station (it's still there) to greet the brave engineer.

Then the wickets banged closed, and George Thomson and his clerks waited for the next action, a horse-drawn sleigh rounding the corner, loaded with mailsacks and clerks who'd been sorting it all the way from Calgary. In their race to Edmonton they tossed off the sacks for Strathcona.

The Strathcona station, as painted by A.B. Cartmell.
Courtesy of the author; used by permission.

Behind bars, George Thomson's four young ladies earned their twenty dollars a month with the final sorting. People formed into lines as they do at the Fringe, in hope and expectation and fear of disappointment. Then the wickets would bang open and there would be letters for some and another wait for others.

The sport ended in 1913. The High Level Bridge opened and CPR trains rattled through Strathcona and over to Edmonton. In the same year, postal service was deprivatized, to a government post office a block west on Whyte Avenue, a structure since converted to bistros and boutiques in a development called Market Square.

The government hired six postmen to deliver letters door to door so there was no longer need to line up at wickets.

Four great clocks in the tower flashed time signals north, east, west, and south, so there was no occasion for the ceremony of consulting watches.

The show was over. But it has echoes today in the Fringe.

19

Queen
City
Saturday
Night

All good things must come to an end, a stern rule of life made milder by the fact that bad things must end too. But with good things it's regrettable that exceptions couldn't be made in extraordinary cases — such as the Saturday night auctions at the Queen City Meat Market.

The meat auctions flourished in the 1920s, made the hungry '30s less hungry, and came to an end with meat rationing in the second world war.

These unique ventures in bargain-and-sale were a personal expression of the founder and proprietor of Queen City — Bill Noak, who was born in Birmingham, England in 1869 and died in Edmonton, Alberta in 1958.

Bill was a stout fellow, built to the cartoon specifications of John Bull and with all the resolution of the breed. Bill liked to do things in a big way and by the turn of the century ran a chain of six butcher shops in his native Birmingham. He liked to deal in quantity, and six shops were certainly that, but he got hold of some figures on the eating habits of North Americans and decided he could sell even greater quantities in America. So in 1910 he was in business in Buffalo, New York.

Bill didn't like the east very much, and when he got hold of figures showing that westerners ate more meat than easterners he was off to Seattle. But Seattle didn't quite suit him, nor did Vancouver, nor did Calgary. Edmonton was a different matter. In 1918, he took the old Bijou Theatre on 100 Street — across from the Market Square, a square since pre-empted by the Milner Library — and transformed our first movie house into the Queen City Meat Market.

Bill made the transformation with lights and white paint, which he liked to see lots of, along with lots of meat. Not for Bill a few lonely steaks in a showcase while a couple of steers hung in the cooler. He liked to see porkchops piled like artichokes on a pushcart. He liked big pieces of meat. He'd rather sell a big chunk of beef and make fifty cents than cut it into three and make a dollar.

In addition to lots of meat, lights, and white paint, he believed in lots of work, walking downtown each morning to open the shop at six o'clock, locking up again fourteen hours later.

He also believed in lots of fun. In Bill Noak's time, men were resigned to being on the job twelve to fourteen hours a day — but they had fun at work. The sausage kitchen behind the shop was a favourite club for judges and great men of the legal profession as they passed up and down 100 Street, to and from the Court House, on the site of today's Edmonton Centre. And if a gathering of great legal minds wasn't cheerful enough, Bill kept a bottle of cheer in his desk.

Queen City delivered meat to any part of the city. Bill enjoyed watching a delivery boy sneak off with a soup bone to trade at a restaurant for a piece of pie.

He had the most fun on Saturday nights when the doors were locked. To end the week he would auction off everything in the shop, free to enjoy an uncluttered Sunday and start the next week fresh.

The auctions began as a spur-of-the-moment thing, on a Saturday on which he'd mixed more fun then usual into the business and faced a large carryover to the next week. He'd often employed auction techniques when business was slow, crossing 100 Street with a platter of lamb chops and strolling through the Market asking for bids.

He put on as fine a show as ever was seen when the shop was the Bijou Theatre: hawking the goods from the top of a counter; holding sausages, chops, and steaks high on platters; reaching under the counter occasionally for that bottle of cheer; singing "Where Did You Get That Hat?", reaching into the crowd for a fancy hat on the head of a lady, and popping it on his own.

Bill's competitors did not take as kindly as the public did to the Saturday soirees. First they sent the police, and the law made Bill lock the doors at six so no one could come in after the close of regular business. Then they sent around the licence inspectors, who made Bill buy an auctioneer's licence.

Auctions are hazardous for impulse buyers. Sometimes people would bid for so many bargains they'd need a taxi to get their treasure home. Then there was the man who bought a twenty-five-pound hip of beef for a dollar and a quarter. He had to get it home — and his home was in Winnipeg.

As the depression sank its great weight on Edmonton, people with big families used to pack the place and get their Sunday dinner — and Monday and Tuesday dinner too — for a dollar. Seven pounds of beef for a dollar.

Bill knew everybody, who was working and who had just been laid off, and when he spotted some discouraged fellow who had just lost his job he'd pick out a fine roast and yell: "Hey ... Joe ... Catch!"

The auctions, governed by the law that all good things must end, were a casualty of the second world war — and rationing. Bill couldn't sell to the highest bidder if the chap didn't have coupons to support his bid. Once coupons began to clutter up the deals, the Queen City auctions were going going gone. Saturday nights have never been the same.

20

Bertie Wooster Lives

It was a shot heard halfway round the world.

In 1956 Lord Tony Vivian, London theatrical producer, was potted by his neighbour, Mrs. Mary Wheeler, in the garden of her home at Davizes, Kent. It was a misunderstanding. Lord Tony had decided to come into the house through a window instead of applying at the door. Not recognizing him in the dark, Mrs. Wheeler potted away with her pistol, and he fell wounded among the flowers.

The shot that dropped Lord Tony inflicted minor damage, but halfway round the world it raised a covey of stories of the roaring twenties when Lord Tony — he was just Honourable then — skylarked about Edmonton with his peers. Chaps like Lord Edward Montague, Owen Crosby, and the Honourable John Hoare — chaps with whom Bertie Wooster might have sported at the Drones Club.

Before the first war and after, sons of the wealthy and influential were farmed out to the colonies to see if they couldn't find something to do. They were nice young chaps. They were well bred. They were well intentioned. They were well liked. They were well educated — but not, alas, to do anything.

The Honourable John Hoare had been sent out to be a farmer, sent to another British peer who'd made a go of it. But his career in agriculture was as brief as it was undistinguished. Dash it all, a chap has to draw the line somewhere and what better place to draw it than at farming in Alberta? Surely a nephew of British financial wizard Montagu Norman could scrounge a living in Edmonton.

John and his pals wore their school ties with distinction, along with their moustaches and plus-fours. They might have worked in banks, but they preferred employment a little zippier than that.

Just for fun, or when short of the ready, they drove taxis. It was exciting enough for an Edmontonian being driven by an heir to a peer of the realm, and their style made it more so. They drove not in the flat Canadian tradition of "Where to?" but in the spirit of the cry "Tally Ho!" — as though they had viewed the fox in the road ahead.

No one thought any less of them for driving taxis. It was understood that *someday* they would have pots of money, although it was equally understood that they didn't have any money *now*. With their good manners, they were welcome everywhere, in particular at a couple of English tea rooms they made into clubs.

In their hours of relaxation, which were many, they sought what was British and best, and lounged about the tea room of Miss Pussy Forsythe, where Pussy's big dogs Zippy and Pepper also lounged and gave a sporting accent to the place.

They also lounged about the tea room of Mrs. Hayward on west Jasper. Mrs. Hayward was a big, handsome Englishwoman who was understood to have pots of money and unlimited credit for young aristocrats — and a handsome daughter as well. In these clubs they could lounge secure all day making conversation straight out of P.G. Wodehouse.

Tony Vivian was thought to be in some sort of newspaper work, although *Bulletin* reporters were rather under the impression that he did something or other around the *Journal* and *Journal* hands were rather under the impression that he did something or other around the *Bulletin*. He was well known to the press as "the Student Prince," for the hero of a popular operetta of that name. He spent much of his time around theatres, playing bit parts with the Alexis B. Luce stock company at the old Pantages. He fell easily into such roles, with the poise, voice, clothes, and classical education of an Eton man. He was at ease in the theatre and indeed, when a certain relative had the good taste to pop off, Tony would come into pots of money and set himself up as a London producer.

Owen Crosby was the quiet man. He was a tallish chap with chestnut-red hair and soft brown eyes of the sort associated with cocker spaniels. He had the correct manner and clothes for any occasion, and the occasion of the week for Owen's set was the Saturday afternoon tea dance at the Macdonald Hotel. There was no one who could dance so well nor talk so charmingly about light subjects. Owen had to chat about light subjects because he really couldn't converse on profound ones.

He was a great favourite, and no one thought less of him when he was caught one night in 1923 trying to burn down a shoe store. Some said Owen had probably done it at the request of the owner, but most said he hadn't done it at all and was taking the rap for someone else — like that chap in *A Tale of Two Cities*, whatever his name was.

Whoever did the job on the shoe store, Owen was given nine months in Fort Saskatchewan for it. When he emerged, he went home to England, and even the police were sorry to see him go. As Chief Shute observed, "He was always square and above board. In his way."

Eventually the young aristocrats drifted away and would have been forgotten — if it hadn't been for the shot heard halfway round the world.

21

Stimmel for Mayor

A **mighty cheer went up** outside the *Journal* building when a vote was counted for Stimmel. That would be Amer Stimmel, the most popular candidate ever to run for mayor of Edmonton — the most popular, if not the most successful.

It was a long time ago, before electronic media brought election results into the home. Those who couldn't stand the suspense till the late-night extras came on the streets could go downtown and watch as a magic lantern in a second-floor window at the *Journal* projected incoming results across the street to a screen on McDougall Church.

A mayor was granted only one year in office then, and Stimmel brightened the campaigns of 1920, '21, and '22.

Amer brought to electioneering the rhythmic chant of the auctioneer, a profession in which he stood at the very top. He knew all the tricks that made the highest bidder go that extra mile and entertained the crowds with off-the-cuff sallies, playing for time in which the highest bidder would panic and go higher than necessary. He was in wide demand for farm auctions. He had a feeling for farm crowds, a product of his upbringing in a German settlement in Iowa, which also gave him a trace of an accent and an Old Country moustache to go with his short, heavy, barrel-chested figure.

Amer Stimmel prospered in a field in which there was strong competition, and his most vigorous competitor was just over the fence.

Amer and Bob Smith had adjoining auction yards on Churchill Square, across from the present library. Bob Smith was a fiery Irishman with hair to match. A low fence separated the rivals. On Saturdays, Stimmel would be up on his platform selling, and Bob and Amer would entertain the crowds throwing insults back and forth. Their chatter would grow more insulting. And then the crowds would get some real entertainment. Sometimes Stimmel would go over the fence to get at Smith and sometimes Smith would go over the fence to get at Stimmel, but whichever way it was, a rousing ruckus was inevitable.

So a universal cheer went up when Stimmel announced that he was a candidate for mayor in 1920. Stimmel would make things hum. At all the meetings, Stimmel got the biggest hand when he stood up to campaign with his "going-going-gone" patter. And he promised the crowds plenty of action if they made him mayor.

Amer was for work. He was going to run retired people out of town. "If a man's not working, he's no good. Send him to Victoria."

He was against voters accepting free rides to the polls from his opponents. "Nobody never gave me nothing except once an aunt in California gave me nine dollars and ninety-five cents."

He was against golf and the city spending money to build municipal golf courses. "You elect Stimmel for mayor and we're not going to spend any more of our taxes so idlers can play cow-pasture pool."

Amer was against figure-jugglers. There was a row over the natural gas franchise, and many candidates spent their allotted platform time hurling figures at each other. "Elect Stimmel for mayor and there won't be no figure-jugglers get past me into the city hall."

He was especially against figure-jugglers who tried to make city-owned utilities look profitable. "If the power plant don't pay, throw it in the river. If the streetcars don't pay, throw them in the river." You could have dammed the river with all the things Amer was going to throw into it.

Stimmel had a classic remark that always brought down the house — and there were so many houses to bring down, with the city arranging eighteen public meetings and the candidates an equal number.

Voters came to these meetings in the mood of theatre patrons to the Klondike Days melodrama. A large lady of British-Imperial mind followed "Fighting Joe" Clarke from meeting to meeting demanding to know whether Joe's running mate George Latham was a member of the Irish Self-Determination Society.

But however unruly the house, Stimmel could bring it down with his classic remark. He'd chant: "This is the most fightinest outfit I've ever seen in my whole life. They get up and they criticize civic affairs. But I'm not going to criticize civic affairs. The way they run 'em at the city hall, I've never been able to find out anything about 'em!"

Like most politicians, Amer Stimmel believed in polls, which he conducted himself and which always showed that Stimmel was a shoo-in. Absolutely everyone he talked to. At the auction yard. In the market across the street. At the hockey games. On the streetcars. On the street corners. In the drug stores where pharmacists were busy filling prescriptions for people who needed whisky for their health. They were all for Stimmel. "We're with you, Amer, boy. Run the retired people out of town. Throw the streetcars in the river. Out with the figure-jugglers and down with cow-pasture pool. We're with you, Amer."

And on election night, when the crowds gathered outside the *Journal*, a great cheer would go up with every vote for Stimmel. But there were so few: 47 one year, 22 another, 255 at best.

"I never knew there were so many blank-blank liars in Edmonton," said the most popular, though not the most successful, candidate for mayor.

22

Riverboat
Days

The river dealt contradicting ends to its two famous steamboats.

In 1899, a flood lifted the *Great Northwest* off the beach of Rossdale, where she had been downgraded to a warehouse, and sent her on a final voyage of disintegration.

In 1917, a sudden drop in water level trapped the *City of Edmonton* in a deathgrip of mud at her dock off Kinsmen Park, ending the boat and the age of steam navigation on the North Saskatchewan.

But it didn't end the career of Walter Leslie, who'd been engineer, mate, and captain of the *City of Edmonton*. Forced ashore, he kept up steam in provincial government buildings for thirty years, and for fifty years was the voice of authority on riding the river, speaking in the misty brogue of his native Orkney Islands.

Walter Leslie came this way in 1910, at the urging of his uncle John Walter, another Orkneyman, who had arrived in 1870 to build York boats for the fur trade. He expanded his shop on Walterdale to lumberyards, coal mines, real estate (he agreed to buy an automobile when he sold $100,000 worth and got a 1912 Case), a power plant that ran the Edmonton street railway, and boats to link his enterprises up and down the river.

A tale of river city. Perhaps 1914 ... John Walter's City of Edmonton *below the Macdonald Hotel. The hotel is a project of the railroads, which will soon end the age of the riverboats.*
Photo courtesy of the author.

The *City of Edmonton*, 132 feet long and paired with smaller *Scona*, was in her second season when Walter Leslie arrived, carrying ten years' experience on salt water — most under sail — fishing and freighting around his native isles and on the world's oceans. Adjusting to a river was a challenge: "That was a bad river to navigate, the Saskatchewan."

The murky surface, always in motion, hid shifting sandbars and unmoving rocks. Low water was a complication. High water was usually a boon, except when smokestacks were laid flat to squeeze under the Low Level Bridge in order to reach the passenger landing. And there were the sudden night fogs. As the boat approached the landing with a load of picnickers from Big Island, the bridge piers would suddenly vanish.

Through the workweek, the boat was a freighter, its big stern wheel churning the thick river down to Shandro Landing, up to John Walter's log booms at Poplar Creek, and beyond to the Rocky Rapids near Drayton Valley. On holidays and weekends, she was transformed to an excursion boat, taking holiday crowds of four hundred up to Big Island or down to Fort Saskatchewan. At a daily operating cost of thirty-five dollars, excursions were good business — so good that the staterooms on the lower deck were ripped out and a maple dance floor laid down. A floor scuffed by sacks of grain coming up from Shandro Landing would be polished smooth again by flying feet.

Fun and games weren't limited to excursions, as Walter Leslie found when he took a crowd of English investors to the Grand Rapids to study a possible site for a hydroelectric dam. Among supplies being stacked on the deck he noted cases of the distiller's art. He urged the leader to stow the whisky in his cabin or the river hogs — the deck hands — would get it. But the warning was dismissed. With touching belief that the sanctity of cargo on Britain's high seas would be respected on colonial rivers, the leader scoffed, "They wouldn't dare touch cargo!"

In the morning his mistake was riotously evident. He wrestled the cook for a bottle and lost. The *Edmonton* had to poke her nose into a bank and tie up for a day while the river hogs slept off the surprise party.

Ottawa was a long way off, which was good news and bad news. On the negative side, federal authorities were supposed to keep the channel free of hazards, but they were too remote to know about a pesky rock in the Blue Rapids. So one day Walter and engineer Henry Berger took fifty sticks of dynamite downriver and ended that rock's career of public mischief.

On the positive side, the fact that the inspectors were a long way off allowed more power for the boats. The engine of the *Scona* came out of an earlier smaller boat called the *Strathcona* and was a little weak for its responsibilities. With no inspectors hanging around, the valves could be tied down when the *Scona* needed extra push or pull. On Mark Twain's Mississippi, tying down valves was a potentially explosive practice resorted to in steamboat races, but men navigating the North Saskatchewan saw safety in short bursts of power that couldn't blow up a boiler. A touring official who inspected the *Edmonton* ruled that the shaft to her paddlewheel was too light for her boiler but went away without sealing the gears, so Walter — and other captains like Pete Christensen and Abe Pearce — had extra pull to get off a sandbar or extra push to drive up through a heavy current.

The *Edmonton* cruised at six knots — seven in clear deep water — burning coal from the Fulton mine, a convenient riverbank colliery at Clover Bar. Although churning upstream was slower, the current was a friend, reducing thrust into a sandbar and helping her pull off. Coming downstream, the current would drive the boat deep across the bar and help keep her there.

Walter once got the *Scona* off an upstream gravel bar while sleeping on his problem. He'd gone overside and dragged a channel from deep water to the boat. While he slept, the river washed the gravel from under the hull, and the *Scona* came whistling into Edmonton shortly behind a party of journalists who were reporting her hopelessly stuck.

Handling a riverboat was a delicate art. The flat bottom drew only eighteen inches, fine for sliding over shoals, but if a sudden crosswind caught the high flat sides, the boat could take off skating like a waterbug. Turning a sternwheeler around was part of the art. A sidewheeler like the *Great Northwest* could reverse one paddle and spin on one of those big Victorian pennies, but a sternwheeler had difficulty even getting around sharp bends. Approaching some hairpins, captains would get turned in a wide piece of river and back into the bend.

Backwards was often the best way to go, if the *City of Edmonton* had a scow or gold-dredge lashed to her bow. A captain backing downstream had better control. Captain Leslie would back from Big Island to Whitemud Creek and about-face in the wide stretch off Fort Edmonton Park. But the manoeuvre was tricky. When the bow began to come around, it swung with a rush.

Walter Leslie said you had to understand the eddies, make them work for you. Old Captain Grant never could. A grand gentleman, master of many oceans, he didn't understand the effect of eddies — or the current either. One day they found him in the wheelhouse steering away for all he was worth — and the boat firmly aground on a hidden sandbar. With the current breaking white over the bows and carrying flotsam past on both sides, Old Captain Grant had to be convinced that he wasn't taking the *City of Edmonton* upstream as ordered.

Flat-bottom boats could range the river without benefit of docks, and in an emergency be ashore in moments, as on a 24th of May when the *Edmonton*, taking a happy picnic crowd to Fort Saskatchewan, hit a rock. The hole in the bow could be repaired easily with oakum and a couple of planks, but that would need several hours and the passengers were impatient. So Walter hiked to the nearest rural telephone and advised his uncle to send the *Scona*. He was cautioned to make two trips with the small boat and rated this a good occasion on which to have the inspectors far off in Ottawa. "When the *Scona* came alongside, the passengers all jumped aboard and I couldna stop 'em."

Picnic crowds were good about paying — they couldn't go aboard without putting down their dollars in advance. But some commercial customers demanded ingenuity — like the Chicago promoter with the gold dredge. All summer, the *City of Edmonton* had been towing it to this and that gravel bar without reward. When the entrepreneur eventually ordered it towed from Big Island back to the landing below the Macdonald Hotel, Walter Leslie showed an ingenious approach to bill collecting.

Off Walterdale, he shut down the engines, tied up in midstream, and advised the promoter in effect that the dredge would stay there till doomsday or the account was settled, whichever came first. The customer did not pay with becoming grace — but he paid.

The *City of Edmonton* survived the high water of 1915, when a June heat wave over the Rockies sent the winter's snow to overwhelm prairie rivers. Pete Christensen was captain that year. As the flood grew menacing, John Walter told him to let the boat go, but Pete was a captain in the finest tradition. He stayed with the ship, keeping up steam and blowing the whistle, in repeated defiance of debris hurtling past — dangerous flotsam that could crush a wooden steamboat. Relentless, the river came over the banks into Walterdale, forcing the evacuation of John Walter's lumberyards and machine shops but presenting an opportunity to save the ship.

When the flood inched high enough, Henry Berger said, "Come on, let's bring her in." With men hauling on ropes and Pete doing his best with steam and wheel, they moved her behind a sheltering carpenter shop and tied her to a tree.

The flood raged on and swept away John Walter's lumberyards — stacks of finished lumber collapsed and floated off piece by piece — but when the river's fury subsided, the *City of Edmonton* was again riding gently at her dock.

In the end, it was low water that got her — in the fall of 1917 while she lay at the dock. Through the fatal night the river fell without warning and dropped her on the muddy bottom. Mud grabbed her hull along the entire length and defeated all efforts to free her.

The Mark Twain superstructure was recycled. Railings made good fences. The maple dance floor, blessed by memories of holiday cruises to Big Island, was put down in the farm home of John Walter's son at Sandy Lake. But the river never released the hull. It's still there off Kinsmen Park.

"That was a bad river to navigate, the Saskatchewan." Walter Leslie knew.

(In assembling this story, I had the kind assistance of Marvin Combs, who shared the tape recordings of his conversations with Mr. Leslie.)

23

Mr. Scotland

In the beginning there were Scots. The Hudson's Bay Company brought them here when George III was on the throne.

The Scots kept coming. In 1864, when Reverend George McDougall opened a school, Gaelic was the language and he introduced the kids to English.

Scots kept coming. Well into the 1950s, the Edmonton telephone book displayed more MacDonalds than Smiths or Joneses.

Many were accorded the honorary title *Scotty*. But only one was Mr. Scotland. That was Tom Campbell, who imprinted his name on a well-known furniture company.

Tom was born at Greenock on the Clyde in 1883. He used to explain, in his soft, compelling voice, that he'd been born in 1883 because the cost of living was cheaper then.

When Tom grew to the age of sixteen, life presented two options. Should he apprentice himself to a carpenter and endure five years of serfdom in the time-honoured Scottish way so that he might style himself a journeyman carpenter? Or should he emigrate to Canada?

He chose the path of adventure and sailed for the new world with the hopes and blessings of his family and his boyhood sweetheart. Well, not quite all his family. Aunt Cattie was against it. Aunt Cattie said Tom should stay and apprentice properly, and issued a doleful warning that if he went to Canada, he'd not be Mr. Scotland: he'd be Mr. Nobody and lucky to be that.

And Tom's first night on land in Quebec City seemed to support Aunt Cattie. He arrived with eight gold sovereigns and was promptly robbed of seven, leaving him with about five dollars to begin his conquest of the new world.

Although not a qualified carpenter by standards of the old world, Tom found he could get plenty of that work in the new, and hammered his way across Canada. He spent seven months in St. Boniface, Manitoba, building the Catholic cathedral; then headed for Lloydminster, walking the last hundred miles ahead of the railroad. There, at age twenty-one, he set himself up as a contractor and soon saved money for a major investment. He sent for his sweetheart, and Helen Gilchrist came out to join him in Lloydminster and in matrimony.

By 1911, Edmonton was in a real estate boom. Tom joined the excitement with the firm of Magrath and Holgate, helping investors plan fortunes — which soon proved the contention of Tom's favourite poet that best-laid plans *gang aft agley*. Tom's thoughts turned again to pioneering and to the Peace River country. He and his pal Dr. Morton Hall thought they might homestead there, and since no railroad was available, they walked, crossing Lesser Slave Lake on ice in November. Tom reported there was certainly plenty of land and it was all free — appealing to a Scot — but there was so darned much it lost its charm.

Back in Edmonton, no one was buying lots or having houses built on them. Tom wangled a scarce job in the land titles office and was glad to get it. But then, in January 1916, he abruptly quit. There had come one of those tides in the affairs of men which, when taken at the flood, lead to fortune. (Tom regretted that the quotation was from a bard other than Scotland's finest, but it was true even if the bard was English.) The *Edmonton Journal* announced a contest: a prize of one thousand dollars to the man who sold the most classified ads.

Tom worked day and night for five weeks and won the prize. Then he risked it all in a manner prescribed by another English bard, Rudyard Kipling. He invested the prize in a furniture business. Campbell's Furniture opened its doors in April 1916 in a wooden building on the present Rice Howard Way. The *Journal's* prize was all the capital he ever put into the business, which, though it left downtown, carried on at a west-end location.

The 1920s brought a rival to newspapers. Radio burst into the lifestyle of the world, and Tom Campbell was one of the first Edmonton merchants to take advantage of it. *The Home Melody Hour* was broadcast on many hundred Sunday afternoons of the 1920s and '30s with Tom as host. He played the most pleasant music available on records of the time. Between records, he was a homely philosopher, and if the philosophy was that of the land of misty glens and Robert Burns, Tom made no apology for that. He'd hired the hall. If you thought some other philosophy was homelier, you could buy your own hour on CJCA.

Tom's business flourished, and as it did, he could give less time to furniture and more to being Mr. Scotland. The St. Andrew's Society organized — Tom was second president. In 1926, the Burns Club organized — Tom was one of the five founders. The Highland Games became the feature of Edmonton's 24th of May holiday, and for eighteen years Tom was chieftain. The games went on at the South Side Athletic Grounds, now the playing fields of Strathcona Composite High School, and were the biggest in Canada. Vancouver claimed bigger crowds but included horse racing, a sideshow rejected by local Scots.

The events required coordination of many elements, of which the caber was a case in point. In prairie air, the caber would dry and crack and lose the prescribed weight for tossing. Tom's pal police Sergeant Alex Riddell had custody of the caber. He preserved its proper qualities by storing it in the duck pond at Borden Park Zoo.

Tom was still Mr. Scotland in 1952 when then-Princess Elizabeth came to Edmonton with the young Duke of Edinburgh. Tom offered to decorate the steps of the legislature for the Princess, and she was greeted by the colourful spectacle of three hundred lassies in traditional costume. The lassies were all of one ethnic group and wore the tartans of the group, but Mr. Scotland saw no reason to apologize for that.

It recalled one of his first triumphs, thirty years earlier, when he and his pals made arrangements for another illustrious visitor, Harry Lauder, the Scottish entertainer. They booked the Victoria Armoury — at 100 Avenue and 106 Street, still a provincial government office — and were happily selling tickets when it occurred to someone that the place had no chairs. It was common knowledge that the public school board had folding chairs — stacks of them. Tom was sent as ambassador, hoping to make the school board a partner in the cultural experience of "Stop Your Ticklin' Jock" and other great songs rendered in person by the composer. Tom made such a mesmerising case that the board gave him three thousand folding chairs — at the Scot's favourite price.

The only problem with being Mr. Scotland was that he could never take a day off, not even at Jasper Park Lodge on a golf holiday with his pal Monsignor MacLellan. Bing Crosby was there too. In his capacity as Tom Campbell, Tom arranged a game with Bing. Then, in his capacity as Mr. Scotland, he had to rustle up a Balmoral cap to present to the king of the crooners as "a welcome to the Highlands of Canada."

Along about 1934, Tom went on a tour of his own — back to the scenes of his youth. He took his big touring car along on the ship; the Packard, and stories of his adventures in the new world, made a suitable impression on old friends and family. Well, not quite all the family. Not Aunt Cattie. The old dear was still around, unmellowed by time, unconvinced that Tom was Mr. Anybody. The Packard and the stories she dismissed with granite-tipped humphs.

Aunt Cattie saved her most indignant humph for the day Tom invited her to go for a drive and have tea with the Duke of Hamilton.

"The Duke of Hamilton. He'll not see *you*!"

Tom wheeled up the drive of the estate which Hitler's deputy Rudolf Hess would make famous with a surprise parachute-jump in World War Two. The functionary who answered Tom's ring seemed on the same wavelength as Aunt Cattie — but did concede there might be a reason, however unlikely, that His Lordship would consent to see Tom.

"See that statue?" said Tom, pointing to a heroic bronze likeness of the original Duke. "I raised a lot of money for that."

The current Duke insisted they come in for tea. Aunt Cattie was overwhelmed. Tom's greatest detractor had to admit that he was indeed Mr. Scotland.

24

Where's
the Fire?

Slim Reigh drove fire engines in the motorized age of Edmonton firefighting, but his rollicking spirit belonged to an earlier time. Many Irishmen are gifted with eloquence. Dublin's Slim Reigh was gifted with volume, so much that he disdained sirens and went racketing through the streets bawling: "Git out the way fer the fire engine! Git out the way fer the fire engine!" And people got.

Slim's gift helped him locate an old friend who had moved to Vancouver. He knew the street but not the address. So he hired a cab, had the cabbie stop in the middle of each block, where he'd get out and call his friend's name. Within a few blocks Slim's pal rushed out to greet him.

Edmonton civic authorities felt Slim's unique warning system detracted from the metropolitan image they were trying to project, but he rejected their concerns. Although Slim was a professional, his spirit would have been at home and at work at the beginning of local firefighting. That was in 1892, when one of the first acts of the newly incorporated town was the purchase of a shining red chemical wagon.

A crowd described as "half the town" went across the river to see the arrival of this wonder at the CPR station — but there was no one to operate it. So a town meeting was called for Pete Daly's drug store, to form a fire brigade and elect a chief. Tommy Lauder was a natural, a once-and-future chief. He later served in a professional capacity and his son Jimmy was chief farther on.

The chemical wagon was housed in a shack about where people enter the Convention Centre today. A giant bell, eight hundred pounds of it, stood on the grass in front to summon volunteers to fight fires. It also sounded the alarm on a crucial night in 1892 to warn residents that a raiding party from south of the river was trying to kidnap the land titles office.

A team of horses was needed to haul the chemical wagon to a conflagration, and since the brigade had no horses in residence, the first man to arrive with a team was paid five dollars for his fast response. The system produced healthy competition and occasional fights when a race ended in a tie.

The next year, 1893, the town fathers invested further in fire protection. They bought the volunteers a steamer — a fearsome thing that belched steam, smoke, and water with equal fury. To keep the monster supplied with water they dug cisterns — eleven of them storing twelve thousand gallons each. And they put up a brick fire hall. It's hard to describe exactly where it was: not only has the building disappeared but so have the streets, under Canada Place.

On the southwest corner of 98 Street and 101A Avenue, the brick building was more than a fire hall. It was a civic everything. The police force worked out of it — his name was Al Patterson. Above the fire station was a hall for meetings of town councillors, who were volunteers like the firemen; for town meetings; for sessions of the supreme court of the Northwest Territories. There were offices for an assessor, a bookkeeper, and a commissioner of works, about all the administration the town needed.

By 1901, growth of the town was expressed by an addition to the fire hall. A two-storey wing provided cells for the police — one notable guest was registered simply as Murderer Bullock. It provided more civic offices, and although a creaky staircase was not in the architectural specifications, it was welcomed by bosses for snitching on employees sneaking in late.

An interior view of Fire Hall Number Three, ca. 1908
Photo from Edmonton Fire Department Souvenir album, 1908; courtesy of the author.

Janitorial service offered an early example of contracting out. Police kept a warrant on hand for a citizen named Pete, a gentleman of no fixed abode, no fixed occupation, and no fixed aim in life. When the place became untidy, they'd go looking for Pete and put him to work mopping, sweeping, or shovelling.

Some paid employees got rent-free room over the fire hall in return for bolstering the brigade when the bell rang. Arthur Ormsby, later a city commissioner, was one. Another was W.H. Clark, founder of the long-lived lumber company.

The year 1903 brought progress for Edmonton and for firefighting: a waterworks with hydrants. But the water failed on a clamorous night in 1906 when Robertson's Hall burned. Robertson's was a famous gathering place just east of today's Convention Centre. Left high and dry, the volunteers showed admirable ingenuity: they requisitioned barrels of beer from the Jasper House (Hub Hotel). But although the contents could quench thirst, they could not quench the flames which sent Robertson's Hall crackling into history.

This was about the last hurrah for the volunteers. Shortly after, a group picture appeared in a streetfront window of the Empire Block, under the pathetic caption "The Men That the City Doesn't Need Anymore." The volunteers had gathered for a final photo opportunity, on news that the proud city of Edmonton was engaging a force of professionals.

In came G.H. Davidson, son of the chief at Sherbrooke, Quebec. In came two dozen professional firefighters, and professional horses too, to staff regional fire halls — in the west end on the site of the Milner Building, in the east end at 96 Street and 105A Avenue.

A horse-drawn wagon departing a fire hall was a noisy case study in coordination of man and beast. The alarm sounded. Men came down a brass pole as harness dropped over horses. Harness was secured. The unit went out the door — all in sixty seconds.

When their flight was in winter, a wild clanging topped up the excitement. Wagons were converted to sleighs. To avert a jerking start, which might throw the sleigh into the side of the doorway, runners were mounted on hundreds of bits of iron pipe, and each bit contributed its own clang.

Spectators cheering the thundering parade recognized the components — the chief in the lead on a one-horse cart, pursued by the chemical wagon and hose wagons. The lads of the chemical wagon made the initial assault on the fire while the hose men hooked up to hydrants. The chemicals were soda water in sixty-gallon tanks — plus acid, which created such a furious fizz that the concoction was projected into the flames.

There was no problem getting horses to a fire. The problem — as Harry Shea explained, and Harry would know, being a contemporary of Slim Reigh — was getting them to stop when they got there.

The work was tougher in winter, toughest for the man who had to stand with the horses while his buddies kept warm fighting the blaze. The horses, having blankets, were better off. Sometimes those who stood and waited crawled under the blankets too.

Except for a half hour of exercise each day, the horses spent their lives inside, pointed towards the doors. Little wonder they were so wildly eager to thunder forth. And their human partners were almost as confined. Married men were allowed out for meals at seven a.m., twelve noon, and six p.m. Bachelors were let out an hour earlier and usually made for the Phoenix Café, the firemen's club, named appropriately for a bird that rose from the ashes. The Phoenix offered companionship and meal tickets — twenty-one meals for five dollars. Benedicts were allowed to sleep at home on their day off; bachelors had to be back in at midnight. A mite medieval, but it was the same everywhere and the pay was good — seventy-five dollars a month.

It was in 1914 that the internal combustion engine began breaking up the unique partnership of man and horse. The department brought in its first truck, and horses faced redundancy.

Fine specimens all, they were in brisk demand and most accepted the change. But not Jock and Minnie, a pair of dapple greys who worked out of the 1893 main hall. They were sold to a farmer at Cooking Lake and employed in the plowing of furrows. That was no life for a firehorse. One night they went over the fence. In the morning, they trotted into the main fire hall and took up their assumed places.

Officialdom took the hint. No more plowing for Jock and Minnie. They were retired to a life of elegant ease on an acreage. It was close to the city, so close that when the wind was right, they might have heard Slim Reigh yelling: "Git out the way fer the fire engine!"

25

Judge
Noel

Our legal fraternity liked to cite the judgements of J.C. Noel, district court judge of the district of Athabasca from 1907 to 1920, judgements in the courtroom and beyond. His district was all of Alberta from the Saskatchewan River to the northern boundary, excepting only the city of Edmonton.

In Judge Noel's time, the territory was passing noisily from wild to pioneer to civilized state. In the confusion, a Solomon was required to make the punishment fit the crime. The peaceful classic traditions of law, in which he was schooled at Laval University, were seldom much help in the judicial district of Athabasca.

Chief Justice O'Connor illustrated the point with a reminiscence of Fort Saskatchewan at the turn of the century. The local lawyer who acted as prosecutor had an overfondness for the distiller's art, which was available at ninety cents a quart with volume discounts. The magistrate felt this impaired the lawyer's ability to present cases for the crown, and on the eve of sessions took to locking him up along with the accused. Townspeople recognized the prudence of the arrangement but sensed an injustice. The Fort's defence lawyer had the same problem. They thought he should be locked up too. And in the exercise of British fairness, he was.

On the surface, Judge Noel seemed out of place. He was asked to take a travelling justice show on the road — the term *road* used very loosely — through a noisy, aggressive hinterland. He was the opposite of noisy and aggressive. Mild and soft-spoken with an old-world gentleness, he bore a notable resemblance to Sir Wilfrid Laurier.

As his judicial district developed, railroad builders made it easier for him to travel. The builders also provided a setting for one of his most-quoted observations. As his train rattled around a curve, a cow came into view, a very contented cow, standing placidly on the track, eating away at the grass which was eating away at the shaky roadbed. The engineer whistled. The cow looked up, saw the train, and all in a single motion jumped off the track. J.C. Noel nodded approval. "She make good judge — make quick decision."

Once a year, in June, he set out on a grand tour of the Peace River country, travelling with the prosecutor, defence lawyers, and clerk of the court. Before the railroads, the tour took two months, beginning with a two-day jolt on a democrat to reach Athabasca Landing.

At the landing, his entourage was in company with hundreds of settlers, fighting for space on the steamboats, trying to expand the frontier to the land of the mighty Peace. The court would be two days on a boat up the Athabasca River to Mirror Landing (now Smith). From there it was up to an irksome fourteen-mile portage, then on to another boat for a trip down to Lesser Slave Lake and to Grouard at the western end. Then an overland safari to Peace River town and more steamboats — up to Dunvegan, three days down to Fort Vermilion, and five days up against the current of the mighty river.

At Grouard, he held court going and coming. Grouard was then a riproaring frontier town with all the props of a western movie set, another staging point for settlers seeking the promised land of the Peace. There was always plenty of justice to dispense at Grouard, and one case produced an often-quoted Noel judgement.

An Indian from Wabasca was charged with stealing a horse. A livery stable owner testified that the accused had been in Grouard a year earlier and, lacking transportation home, had taken a horse from the stable and hadn't returned it. The prosecutor argued that the accused had kept the horse for a year. That seemed rather longish time to keep it if he didn't intend to steal it. But Judge Noel had reasonable doubt of intent. "Ah well," he said, "what's time to an Indian?"

But once he convicted an Athabasca man on what everyone agreed was weak evidence. Afterwards, he was having lunch with his entourage, including the defence counsel, Harry Robertson, the leading criminal lawyer of the day.

"Judge," said Harry, "I suppose he was probably guilty, but I don't understand how you convicted on that evidence."

"Ah," replied the judge with a grave twinkle, "whatever doubt I might 'ave 'ad was resolved by da fact dat 'e brought you all de way 'ere to defend 'im — da most eminent criminal lawyer in da country — I felt 'e mus' be guilty."

The unique wisdom of Judge Noel surfaced at St. Paul in the case of a man accused of stealing a pig. He convicted the man and then suspended sentence. The prosecutor objected that the culprit was being allowed to pay his debt to society too easily. The judge gave his most ingratiating smile: "Oh, but she was such a leetle peeg!"

People enjoyed the judgement he passed on a newcomer at a social function — a gushy young man full of advice on how things ought to be done in the west. J.C. Noel became more and more irritated. Finally he said: "My fran, w're you come from?" The newcomer said he was from Toronto, intimating that Toronto's loss was Edmonton's gain. "Oh well, you live a righteous, God-fearing life and people will forget it."

People also enjoyed the case in which he was obliged to find himself guilty — of forgetting an arrangement. It was made on the primitive road to St. Albert where he was travelling with the prosecutor and a lawyer named "Slops" Dunlop to try a young man accused of stealing a sheep and converting it to his own use. "Slops" was acting for the defence. All agreed they'd like to get back to the city early for a big social event. "Slops" suggested a way. He would confine his defence to a few minutes if the judge would suspend sentence. The prosecutor liked the plan. He made a few remarks on behalf of His Majesty the King, "Slops" made a few in rebuttal — then Judge Noel forgot the script.

He gave the thief three months. "Slops" was aghast. He whispered about the arrangement and suggested that the client's family would think he had put up a very bad defence. Judge Noel's eyebrows shot up in Gallic horror. Then his eyes melted in Gallic charm.

"Haa ... Don' worry, my fran, I will make it right for you." Radiating warmth, he went to the back of the courtroom where the family was eyeing daggers at "Slops." But he made it right. "Ah my frans ... you say da counsel for defence did not make a long speech. 'E talked for a leetle and I gave him three months. But if 'e 'ad talked longer I should have given seex months."

Judge Noel died in 1920. Shortly before, he gave a summary of his philosophy in the corridor of the Edmonton Court House. A young lawyer had just been admitted to the bar. Emerging from the ceremony, he showed his diploma. The judge smiled. "'Ow long it take you to get dat t'ing?" Four years, he was told. "Ha. Take you longer'n dat to get over it."

26

Graydon's Drug Store

George Graydon was discouraged. It was January 1894. He had come to Edmonton to run a drug store and his first impressions of the town had laid his spirits low.

His predecessor Peter Ross had gone broke and the principal creditors, Bole Wynn and Co., had persuaded George to go out from Winnipeg and succeed where Peter had failed.

He went with reluctance, and the look of Edmonton and its twelve hundred people did nothing to shake his pessimism. Not even all the metropolitan happenings reported by the *Bulletin* convinced him that this was a go-ahead place.

The issue of January 15, which reported Mr. Graydon's arrival, also reported that the train had left Calgary on time.

It announced that the WCTU would put on a temperance entertainment at Robertson's Hall Tuesday next — "an interesting program will be rendered" — and there was a story about W. Vogel who "caught a live eagle at Rabbit Hill last weekend. The eagle was so overloaded with rabbit it had been eating that it could not take off and Mr. Vogel ran it down on foot."

Among the advertisements were fifteen items about stray cows and horses. So it will be obvious to you, as it was to the editor of the *Bulletin*, that Edmonton was bustling place destined for commercial greatness. Strangely, it was not apparent to George Graydon. Even the prospect of the temperance entertainment Tuesday next failed to cheer him. Then a man drove past the drug store on a dray.

He had a cheerful, confident air. "Who's that?" Mr. Graydon inquired.

"That's Abe Cristall, the first Jewish merchant in town. He came here last fall."

"Well now, Abe's people never make a mistake about business. If Abe stays, there's a future here."

Abe Cristall stayed, and so did George Graydon; and through forty-six years he made Graydon's Drug Store part of the life experience of generations of Edmontonians. A step inside was a step back into the nineteenth century, of which the proprietor was an unyielding representative: a dim world of fumed oak cabinets, chairs with thin wire legs, and ruby-hued bottles with shapes of the Arabian Nights ranged on the shelves that stretched up and away to the fourteen-foot ceiling.

The bottles, whose colours grew subtle with age, were to a druggist what red, white, and blue poles were to a barber. To the dean of Alberta dispensers, as he soon became, pharmacy was a calling complete unto itself. When the Owl Drug Store — at First and Jasper — installed a fashionable soda fountain, George Graydon took the marble counter as an affront to the profession.

He didn't say much, of course. He never said much about things that concerned him personally. It was some time before Edmonton learned anything of his earlier life. That he'd been born in St. Catherines, Ontario, in 1857; that he was a graduate of the Ontario School of Pharmacy; that his first wife had died and he'd come west to forget, joining the Mounted Police at Regina and serving at base hospitals during the Riel Rebellion; that he had married Rose Woodward, daughter of the first landowner in Regina; that he'd moved to Winnipeg and then to Edmonton, where the continued presence of Abe Cristall told him he should stay.

Graydon's drug store number one.
Photo courtesy of the City of Edmonton Archives EA 255-24; used by permission.

That decision meant he was here for Edmonton's first Klondike Days, helping the original cast outfit themselves for the journey north. His big seller with the gold rush crowd was instant tea. Many people today believe that all things instant are new ideas. But instant tea came in cubes — in tins — and Graydon the druggist supplied many a tin to Klondikers. Unfortunately, the gold rush ran out before the stock of instant tea, and for years after the Graydon family was drinking it up.

In the days of the Klondike, the store was on the south side of east Jasper Avenue, on the Convention Centre site. The family lived upstairs, where second-storey windows gave Mrs. Rose Graydon views of scenes she didn't care for and led to some of that social activism by which pioneer women were making the frontier a kinder, gentler place.

Out the back windows, she overlooked a corral where horse dealers broke Indian ponies in what Mrs. Graydon considered a cruel and sadistic manner. When the whinnies of pain and fear grew too distressing, she called the police. (There couldn't be a corral there now — the cliff top has slipped down Grierson Hill.)

Out the front windows, she gained a disapproving view of social life at the Alberta and Queens hotels. On cold winter nights, when revellers disappeared into hotel bars and left their poor horses shivering, Mrs. Graydon would summon the police, who put the horses in livery stables. The owners had to pay stable charges to get them out and were downright nasty about having their horses towed away, but Mrs. Graydon didn't give a cube of instant tea for their rage. The police chief made her an honourary member of the force with a regular police badge, and horses were towed away in greater numbers yet. In 1903, she was a founder of the Edmonton Humane Society, which in 1912 became the Society for Prevention of Cruelty to Animals.

With the new century, George Graydon moved his stock west along Jasper to the Sandison Block, where Macdonald Place stands today. His family couldn't live above that shop. The second storey was a hall, rented for a host of activities, including those of the supreme court of the Northwest Territories.

In 1905, he stood calm among his medicines, compounding and dispensing while the murder trial of Charlie King, the most sensational of the era, went on over his head. The city grew around him and changed, traffic in the windows went by faster, trendy competitors put in soda fountains. But he remained firmly in step and in tune with the nineteenth century, right into the second world war, giving the kids the experience of an old-world apothecary and gravely working mortar and pestle in an aura of bottles that glowed in the dimness. That's what people are remembering when they speak of Graydon's Drug Store.

27

First
and
Jasper

While Jim Smith's motorcycle gang represented traffic control in its mobile aspect, the stationary mode meant Tom Adams and Sam Kennedy.

For twenty years, Tom and Sam conducted traffic through First and Jasper. From 1913 to 1933, they got to know more people by sight — and vice versa — than anyone else ever did.

Everybody went through their crossroads. People had to go downtown then: to shop at a department store, see a doctor, see a lawyer, see a dentist, buy a school text, a suit, a coat, a phonograph record — even to see a first-run movie.

All streetcar lines went through First and Jasper. There were only six, not counting the stub lines to Glenora and McKernan Lake, not enough to need numbers. Destinations were identified by coloured signs on the lower right front of the cars — uncomplicated colours — blue, white, blue and white, red, red and white, red and green.

Twelve hours a day, Monday to Saturday, spring, summer, and fall, Tom and Sam stood in the eye of the intersection, waving. They weren't out on Sunday — there wasn't enough traffic to need control — nor in winter, when many automobiles were put up on blocks and they patrolled regular downtown beats.

Sam Kennedy came to the police force in 1910, and his first assignment was traffic at Jasper and 100 Street. Motor cars were just coming into the mix. The province of Alberta had licensed 425 of the things, and a good 200 were in Edmonton.

Sam was a Scot by way of Bruce County, Ontario, who spoke and wrote Gaelic. Tom Adams was a Scot by way of Aberdeenshire and the Glasgow metropolitan police force, and arrived in 1912, the big year of Edmonton's first boom. McDougall Hill was clogged with wagons bringing up the building blocks of the surging city. Tom was put on McDougall Hill, where he was not so much a conductor as an ombudsman, helping sort out the flow. It was often snarled and the teamsters snarly, especially when the grade was slippery with rain. Horses weren't strong enough to bring gravel up the incline, so oxen were pressed into service. For extra traction, they were actually shod — on the rear hooves.

The year 1913 brought a major change in the city's traffic patterns. The High Level Bridge opened, taking a load off McDougall Hill and the beasts of burden. And Tom Adams and Sam Kennedy began their unique partnership at First and Jasper.

Each had his own conducting style for the basic gestures of traffic control — the upraised palm and the beckoning arm sweep. Friends in the city engineering department liked to invent mechanical aids to assist them. There was a device with two arms — one saying STOP, the other GO. There was a box mounted on a stand, with GO on two faces and STOP on the others. It was controlled by a lever. A yank on the lever and Jasper Avenue traffic would be ordered to STOP and First Street invited to GO.

These inventions didn't work very well at night, so the engineers came up with a kerosene lamp illuminating red and green slides.

In all their era, Tom and Sam issued only one ticket. They preferred lectures. Offenders were hailed and bawled out. Sam gave the only ticket — in response to overwhelming public demand. A foolhardy unfortunate made a sweeping left turn, against and through two lanes of approaching traffic. Sam could see that the angry mob wouldn't be satisfied with a lecture and reluctantly wrote a citation.

There was only one interruption in their act. One winter night, Tom was investigating a suspicious movement in the lane behind the CPR building. As he moved in towards a tailor shop, a concealed gunman pumped no less than six slugs, all of which found a target in various areas of Tom. To the surprise of no one but the gunman, Tom survived. He was able to sound the alarm, and his assailant was caught. John Michaels, the presiding genius of Mike's News Stand, raised a fund to send Tom home to recuperate. And after four months of bracing Scottish air, he was back conducting at First and Jasper, nodding to gentlemen and waving to ladies.

Gun toters were an occupational hazard, but the constant worry was runaways. Horses enjoyed the right-of-way over motor cars: a runaway team had better have clear passage through First and Jasper or a horrible splintering collision was almost guaranteed.

From their vantage point in the middle of the road, they would have first view of a runaway. If Sam looked up First Street and observed a wildly snorting team bearing down, he'd whistle and wave with all his might to try to freeze traffic on Jasper.

If Sam hadn't time to get clear himself, he'd jump behind his last line of defence, the steel pole in the middle of the intersection. For many years it was the only steel pole in the city, called on to bear such a weight of trolley wires that the street railway splurged thirty-two dollars for steel. Sam knew that if anything crashed into the pole, it would go no further.

In 1914, their friends the city engineers incorporated the pole in an invention to shield them from the elements — a sort of wooden umbrella to baffle rain and sun. It was hung on the pole, designed so streetcars had clearance, and it worked for a week or so. Then entered an element which hadn't been considered. A gust of wind blew down First Street and spun the umbrella a few degrees on its axis. A streetcar rumbled past and crunched it on one side. A car rumbled by in the opposite direction and crunched the other side. By the time half a dozen cars had had a go at it, the umbrella was mangled beyond recognition and repair.

Eventually all traffic swirls through First and Jasper. But it's under control. Either Tom Adams or Sam Kennedy is in the eye of the swarm.

So they stayed in the open for twenty years, becoming sights as familiar and changeless as the buildings that marked their corner. The Selkirk Hotel. The old Bank of Montreal, three storeys of grey stone with pillars. The old Empire Block, four storeys of purplish brick with Ligget's drug store and soda fountain on the ground floor. Only the northwest corner saw change, the Dominion Cigar Store giving way to the Bank of Commerce.

Tom Adams and Sam Kennedy stood out there, season after season, nodding to gentlemen, bowing to ladies, till the engineers bought an invention surpassing the kerosene signal box and the wooden umbrella. In 1933, Edmonton installed its first electric traffic lights.

28

Heiminck

Versus

the Town

The case of Heiminck versus the town occupied various courts for three and a half years, pitting the town of Edmonton against one of the most crafty and resourceful of its two thousand residents.

Phil Heiminck was a dealer — in anything capable of being bought and sold — and seldom came out second best in a deal. Phil was best explained to newcomers with a story recounted by a gentleman who approached him on the street one day.

"Mr. Heiminck, I have a little account I'd like to collect."

Phil cupped his ear with a pudgy hand. "Eh? What's that?"

Raising his voice the gentleman said, "I have a little account I'd like to collect."

"Eh, what's that?"

(Louder) "I have a little account I'd like to collect."

"Eh, what's that?"

(Louder still) "I have a little account I'd like to collect."

"Eh, what's that?"

Turning away in resignation the gentleman said, "Oh well, I guess I'll go have a drink."

"Good idea," said Phil Heiminck. "I'll join you."

It was hard to come out ahead of Phil Heiminck on a deal, and he had so many of them. He owned land and was agent for much more, including the holdings of Dave McDougall. Dave's father, the Reverend George, had claimed River Lot 6, from 100 Street to 101st and back to 111 Avenue, on behalf of the Methodist Church. Dave claimed adjoining River Lot 8, from 99 to 100 Street, on behalf of himself.

The case of Heiminck versus the Town was fought over Block X of Dave McDougall's claim. From the earliest beginnings of the town there had been an unofficial public market on Block X, and a trail meandering across it called Cliff Street, named for its proximity to the cliff.

Phil sold many lots on the Jasper Avenue side of Block X. In January 1895, he decided the Town should buy the remainder and make it officially a public market, and should also buy Cliff Street.

Town council's reaction was as chilly as the January weather. So, on the second last day of the month, Phil served formal notice: if the council would not buy Block X including Cliff Street, he would barricade the road.

Phil was advised to seek a place considerably warmer than Edmonton in January — the street was a public thoroughfare and couldn't be closed. Phil was dared to barricade the street.

This he promptly did. On February fourth, he put up a stout fence. In bad old days of claim-jumping, thirteen years before, a structure that offended Edmonton's sense of fair play was heaved over the cliff. And history was repeated two days later by order of works commissioner Arthur Ormsby. The fence went down the slope. The road was open. The matter was closed.

But that would have meant that Heiminck was coming out second best. He talked it over with lawyers. Granted, he had to go to Calgary to find lawyers who would touch the case, but out of their meetings was born the case of Heiminck versus the Town.

Cliff Street remained open while the matter was theoretically "before the courts," but a full ten months dragged by before the case actually saw a courtroom. Not till December 13, 1895 — Friday the thirteenth — did Mr. Justice Scott get around to hearing arguments in old Robertson Hall. He heard three days' worth and went away to Calgary, and a hockey rink was built on Block X.

In April 1896, the judge was back to hear more cases. When someone asked about Heiminck versus the Town, he said he hadn't decided. It wasn't till July that he did — in favour of the Town.

That should hold Heiminck, thought the Town, but Phil's response was "Eh, what's that?". His Calgary mercenaries were instructed to take the case to the appeal court of the Northwest Territories.

Another year dragged by. The high court came down on the side of the Town.

Surely that'll hold Heiminck, thought the Town, but his response was again "Eh? What's that?". His legal team took the case to the Supreme Court of Canada, which, a year and a day after the territorial court ruled for the Town, ruled for Heiminck.

On June 15, 1898, three and a half years after it all began, the Town was ordered to pay Phil Heiminck five hundred dollars for lawyers' fees and two hundred for the fence it had so rudely uprooted.

Phil could hear that all right, but he didn't do anything except pocket the money. He wasn't really interested in closing Cliff Street — just determined not to come out second best in the deal.

And he was busy with other deals, like putting a public market on the block of Dave's property where the Milner Library stands today. And in 1912, the Town, grown to a City, was happy to close Cliff Street — so the Grand Trunk Pacific Railway could build the Macdonald Hotel.

29

Turn on
the Heat

Edmonton played an exceptional role in the saga of Cyrus Eaton, a ninety-six-year success story stretching from Pugwash, Nova Scotia in 1883 to Cleveland, Ohio in 1979.

Young Cyrus had thought of the ministry, growing up on the north shore. When he was seventeen, he went to Cleveland to live with an uncle who was a renowned minister, but the uncle had a parishioner named Rockefeller. One summer, Cyrus had a job on John D's estate and realigned his priorities.

He quickly showed the Rockefeller touch. By 1912, when he was twenty-nine, he was consolidating small gas companies in the American midwest. By 1923, he was president of United Light and Power, with holdings of $575 million in a dozen states, and he financed many of the mergers through his own bank. It's handy to have your own when other bankers don't share your vision.

In 1926, he organized Continental Shares, which in three years held assets of $100 million in varied enterprises. Over bitter opposition from eastern steel interests, he got into that and by 1930 had gained control of enough companies to form Republic Steel, the third largest. To supply his steel mills he organized the Cliffs Corporation with six iron mines.

In 1929, he took on big rubber, buying into Goodyear, Firestone, and U.S. Rubber. The Wall Street crash, later that year, cost him much of his empire but not his personal fortune, and his next campaign was to free the midwest from eastern domination represented by Wall Street.

The second world war gave Cyrus Eaton a chance to show what he could do for his two countries and for himself. Iron ore was in desperate shortage. He bought the Steep Rock property in northern Ontario for $20,000 cash. The ore was proven but lay under a deep lake in a remote area. To bring it into tank assembly lines, he got $5 million from the American government and Canada built him a road, a railroad, and a dock, also worth $5 million.

The postwar period opened more opportunities. Henry Kaiser, the builder of liberty ships, went into auto manufacturing, financed by Cyrus Eaton's bank. And when industry giants tried to freeze Kaiser-Frazier out of steel, Cyrus organized a steel company to outmanoeuvre them.

Then came the Cleveland Cliffs Corporation, a giant conglomerate, a vehicle for Eaton's further exercises in success.

As Cyrus Eaton passed three score and ten, he was doing a lot of thinking — about ideas like opening up trade with the Soviet Union. In 1954, he invited the top thinkers on the continent to join him at his native Pugwash for a think-in. When it was done, they all said the thinking had been fine and they'd like to come again, which they did year after year, making Cyrus Eaton's hometown synonymous with economic brainstorming.

He went on till 1979, seldom out of the public eye, and when he finally closed his career, his résumé was success on a monumental scale. But there was an exception, an exception full of possibilities, early in his résumé. It happened in Edmonton.

It was 1907 and Cyrus was twenty-four. He had risen quickly in the East Ohio Gas Company, from explaining to angry householders why the company was digging up lawns to scouting the Canadian prairies for franchises his company might acquire.

But while he was in Edmonton, East Ohio fell victim to the financial panics of 1907. Cyrus was stranded without an employer, left with only his infectious self-confidence, his mesmerizing salesmanship, and his

Bluenose ingenuity. Freed of his employer, he could seek a gas franchise of his own — which he did.

Reporters, city councillors, voters — all were intrigued by young Cyrus and his plan to provide Edmonton with gas heat. There was an abundance of petroleum gas in the ground, but his scheme didn't involve anything so unimaginable as that. In many places, gas was manufactured from coal, but he didn't propose anything so unoriginal as that. No, he was going to make gas out of straw, the ordinary straw he observed lying on farms around Edmonton, useless remains of the district's fabulous grain crops.

He could see a vast supply of the stuff, and as land towards all horizons was cleared for more farms, the supply would be endless.

It was technically feasible to make straw into gas. Cyrus was doing it at a small pilot plant in Strathcona, willing to let anyone watch and answering questions, talking about his enterprise which bore the modest name of International Heating and Lighting Company.

And he wrote letters, gingery, bright-eyed letters, urging straw gas on civic authorities — above a signature which was almost a self-portrait, a pictograph of a young man in a hurry, running with long confident strides up an incline, straining forward to snatch success.

With wile and style, he pursued the franchise, and he wasn't alone. The North West Oil and Gas Company wanted to heat Edmonton with natural gas out of the ground. North West wanted an exclusive franchise; Cyrus said straw was such a good deal he would risk competition. Natural versus artificial. The contest produced enough heat to keep a neighbourhood of houses comfortable in January.

Edmonton's city fathers decided to send the contest to a plebiscite. On June 1, 1907, voters who held property rejected natural gas 670 to 325 and went for straw 1083 to 124.

Strathcona fell into Cyrus' pocket. He announced that two hundred men would soon be at work on the $300,000 project. He seemed to have it made. His plan had been ratified by technical experts, city councils, and voters. Unfortunately, there was one more hurdle: it had to be ratified by the farmers. They must agree to keep on supplying straw for almost nothing. They burned it anyway just to get rid of it, but if Cyrus was going to make a buck out of their straw, they wanted in.

The price went up. The concept was no longer viable. But the author didn't pine. He went back to Cleveland and made millions and millions and millions of dollars. And one must wonder: if he had succeeded in Edmonton, would the world ever have heard of Cyrus Eaton?

30

Theatre
Within
Theatre

The play within a play is one thing. Theatre within theatre is another. There was plenty of that in the boom years before the first world war, when Edmonton was on the route of the great vaudeville circuits and dramatic stock companies from the British Isles.

Theatre within theatre occurred at the old Empire on 103 Street one matinee when Norval McGregor deviated from the script by Ibsen. Many British thespians have come to Edmonton to adjudicate actors. On this occasion, Mr. McGregor decided to adjudicate the audience. The play was *A Doll's House*, perhaps a trifled advanced. Mr. McGregor was propounding an Ibsenism to his leading lady, Miss Hortenze Nelson, when loud guffaws erupted in a section of the audience. He left Miss Nelson lying on the couch, stalked down to the footlights, and informed the customers if there was anymore of THAT, he'd dashed well bring down the curtain and they could all dashed well go home.

There was theatre within theatre one night when Sir Harry Lauder, king of Scottish comedy, played the old Empire. A porous roof failed to contain a summer downpour, and rain was soon falling on Harry's

Caledonian parade. But he was equal to the intrusion. He stopped his song and announced: "Keep calm, ladies and gentlemen ... keep calm ... they're lowering the lifeboats!"

Careers also provided theatre within theatre. Sarah Bernhardt, the Divine Sarah, played the Empire at the end of hers, in *Camille*. Charlie Chaplin clowned at the beginning of his; teenaged Fred and Adele Astaire danced at the beginning of theirs. Texas Guinan made a career change. In the roaring twenties of New York's prohibition era, she became queen of the speakeasies with her famous greeting "Hello, sucker!", but in 1901 she appeared at the Empire as a demure heroine in a trendy operetta called *The Gay Musician*. A year later she was back, perhaps slightly less demure, as *The Kissing Girl*.

The Harold Nelson company was the first of the travelling groups, playing Robertson's Hall, above Sheriff Robertson's store, before that wooden landmark burned down in 1906. The company came from Winnipeg, a generation older as cities went, to offer the works of Shakespeare and the contemporary Irish upstart George Bernard Shaw.

Pauline Johnson, the Indian poet, used to bring her one-woman show to Robertson's. She liked to stand on the sidewalk down front watching the parade on Jasper Avenue, much as her sculptured image now gazes out from Vancouver's Stanley Park. One day, in late winter, she observed a dog team arrive from the north with a load of furs for McDougall and Secord. She was touched by the driver, haggard and drawn with the stress of running the dogs to Edmonton before spring thaw. The drama made such an impression that before her night's performance Pauline Johnson had written *The Train Dogs*, one of her most effective pieces.

A few years later, Sir John Martin-Harvey, the great English actor, used to look for theatre over on 102 Avenue, watching settlers load wagons for the Peace River country and other points north. He would stand spellbound and inform all in range of his rich voice, "This is the beginning of things. Here we stand at the beginning of things."

Other great names appeared on playbills here. Forbes Robertson in *The Passing of the Third Floor Back*. Margaret Anglin in *Green Stockings*. Maude Adams in *Peter Pan*. Robert Mantell in one of the first modern-dress *Hamlet*s. Alfred Lunt before Lyne Fontanne. De Wolfe Hopper in

Gilbert and Sullivan, with his curtain-call recitation of *Casey at the Bat*, a unique piece of theatre within theatre.

Stage people had their hotel — the Springer — on 105 Street where the Ramada Renaissance stands now, a family establishment run by Gottbold and Antoinette Springer, who became parents-in-law of Edmonton's pioneer radio broadcaster Dick Rice.

In 1914, the guestbook offered theatre within theatre. Mr. and Mrs. Lawrence Irving were appearing here in *The Typhoon*. People wanted to entertain the son of famous Sir Henry Irving, but he was too busy, working feverishly in his room at the Springer on a play about Napoleon which he hoped to produce in London in the fall. He kept at it, and the Irvings finally hurried away to Montreal to catch the *Empress of Ireland* — a ship marked for doom. Passing Rimouski, the *Empress* rammed a coal ship in fog and went down in fifteen minutes, taking eleven hundred lives. Lawrence Irving, his wife, and the play he was writing at the Springer Hotel were lost — to become legends of the theatre.

Edmonton once knew a night of total theatre within theatre. It began on the evening of July 2, 1907 and extended through to sunrise on the third. On that night, Minnie Maddern Fiske, reigning queen of the American stage, brought her play *The New York Idea* for one performance at the Thistle Rink.

The gala experience was arranged by the Exhibition Association, to give a boost to fair week and demonstrate that Edmonton's boom was run on New York-size ideas. The show had to be at the Thistle Rink (on 102 Street, site of Manulife East) because it was the biggest hall in town, host to several triumphal occasions, including the grand official opening of the first Alberta Legislature.

The play had been the hit of the previous winter on Broadway. Mrs. Fiske brought the original cast, including a rising young British actor named George Arliss.

The performance was to begin at eight-thirty p.m. The train carrying the props arrived at the south-side station on time, two hours before curtain. Sets were lavish and many. A lineup of horse-drawn wagons waited to receive them. Stagehands fell to filling the wagons, theatre within theatre enjoyed by an appreciative crowd.

The wagons moved off down Whyte Avenue — and then more theatre within theatre. The blue skies of sunny Alberta can turn soggy at the most embarrassing times. Wagons were impeded by a chain of quagmires, stretching all the way down Whyte Avenue, 99 Street, Scona Hill, up McDougall Hill, and right to the rink.

By seven o'clock, the cream of Edmonton's young society was gathering at the Thistle, more theatre within theatre as young women in New York fashions trod the boards — of the sidewalk — skillfully avoiding the mud.

At curtain time, the props were still south of the river, accompanied by crowds enjoying the drama of wagon versus sinkhole. Nine o'clock passed. Nine-thirty. But no one minded, least of all Mrs. Fiske and her company. They were loving the novel adventure and the surprising endless twilight. From time to time, someone would mount the stage with a bulletin on the props' progress, assuming the mantle of the butler who announces, "My lord, the carriage waits."

Ten o'clock came. And went. Eleven o'clock. At the witching hour of midnight, the curtain rose. Caught up in the excitement, the reigning queen of the stage gave *The New York Idea* her finest performance.

The July sun was rising when the curtain came down and the audience pressed out to their favourite cafés, where midnight suppers they'd reserved were still waiting. As the sun rose higher, they went home to bed, some to a tent in the woods. But they were content. They had known a total night of theatre within theatre.

31

The
Carruthers
Touch

J.R. Carruthers made his mark on Edmonton through aviation and caveation — and if it is argued that there's no such word as *caveation*, it may also be argued that there is now.

In aviation, his touch was that biplane of the first world war that hung in the Edmonton Convention Centre for ten years.

The war was not a government monopoly — private enterprisers could play a role. Hamilton Gault Barracks, at CFB Edmonton, commemorates the Montreal tycoon who raised Princess Patricia's Canadian Light Infantry and equipped the battalion out of his own large pocket. James Carruthers, also of Montreal, believed in aviation. He helped the government produce pilots by paying for training planes. The best in the air was a Curtiss biplane, whose designation JN-4 made it inevitably "the Jenny." A Jenny cost $7,600. Carruthers thought air-minded cities would like to join him in the cause, buying planes which would be named for donor cities. He invited Edmonton because he'd put the subdivision of Glenora on the real estate market in the boom which was flattened by the war.

Edmonton's response was neither gracious nor encouraging. His letter came to council on the night of September 11, 1917, where it was moved by Alderman MacDonald, seconded by Alderman Bush, "that this communication be filed." No reply. Just filed.

Mr. Carruthers tried again, with an appeal through the Canadian Aviation Fund. It came to council on February 12, 1918, where it was moved by Alderman Kinney, seconded by Alderman Grant, "that this communication be filed."

Disappointed but not bitter, Mr. Carruthers presented a number of Jennies to the government and named one *City of Edmonton*. When war ended, the government gave them back. Despite previous rebuffs, he wrote again, offering the *City of Edmonton* as a gift. That was more like it. Council agreed without dissent. The plane was leased to Wop May and George Gorman, two combat pilots home from France. Gorman flew it to Wetaskiwin and dropped a bundle of *Edmonton Journal*s over the side to record the first commercial flight in Alberta. The *City of Edmonton* barnstormed on weekends, took people up at country fairs, and after many adventures and misadventures ended up on Jasper Avenue — under glass.

As the Carruthers Jenny hung over crowds entering the Convention Centre, the Carruthers Caveat hangs over Glenora, which he acquired from the original owner, Malcolm Groat, in 1906.

Malcolm was, in a sense, the original Edmontonian. On completing his twenty years' service with the Hudson's Bay Company in 1870, he elected not to go home to his native Scottish Isles. He decided that Edmonton was home and claimed the first river lot west of the Hudson's Bay Reserve, which became known as the Groat Estate.

Mr. Carruthers picked the heart of the estate, bounded on the east by Groat Ravine, on the north by Stony Plain Road, on the west by 136 Street, on the south by the river cliffs, and named it Glenora.

He didn't put Glenora on the real estate market right away. He waited till the time was ripe, which he identified as 1911, and when Glenora hit the market there was none of the rowdy hucksterism that attended the entry of surefire money-makers like Jasper Place, Idylwylde, Lauderdale, and Neralcam. (Bonnie Doon shopping centre now occupies all of Neralcam. The real estate team of R.V. MacCosham and P.R. Gaboury got this narrow strip of farm on the market by persuading the Calgary owner — a man named Maclaren — to subdivide it and give it his own name backwards.)

Lots in Glenora were not intended to be sold, turned over at a quick profit, and turned over again at yet another quick profit. They were for building, and the homeowner's investment would enjoy two protections engineered by Mr. Carruthers and his Edmonton agent.

The first was legal, the caveat, binding in law what would never happen in Glenora. No school would ever be allowed, no store would ever be allowed, and no house could ever be built for less than a specific amount — an amount guaranteed to confer the term "posh" on addresses in Glenora.

Second was a prize won in competition among developers. Promoters of raw new subdivisions like the Highlands, Inglewood, and Bonnie Doon knew the first government of Alberta was seeking a location for Government House. The district with the vice-regal palace would have a surefire selling point: "My neighbour, the lieutenant-governor!" Some class to that!

Mr. Carruthers won the prize for Glenora with an offer the province could scarcely refuse, and Government House opened in 1912, built of the same sandstone as the Legislature and two vanished landmarks, the Court House and the Imperial Bank.

James Carruthers was seldom in Edmonton in person, but we saw much of his brother George, who had a specialty. James' talent was making money; George's was spending it. He was often here visiting, getting money from brother James' agent, H.B. Round.

And thereby hangs a tale.

Glenora conferred a happy ending on the long hard-luck story of Henry Barrington Round. The story began in a very English way, a very Victorian way, early in the 1870s, when Malcolm Groat was settling in on his original claim of Glenora.

Henry Round had completed his education, except that he had not seen a colony, and a Victorian Englishman was expected to sample one of Britain's colonies before he called himself educated.

So he went to Montreal and got a job as bank clerk. But that didn't seem "colonial" enough, so he signed on with the Hudson's Bay Company for a tour of duty in the great northwest. The company sent him to Fort Hay River on Great Slave Lake. About the same time, fate sent him a bride.

She was Frances Anne Wheelwright, daughter of a colonel in Britain's Indian army. Her family were friends of Bishop Bumpas, the dear old Anglican church leader. The Bumpases were leaving England for a tour of western Canadian missions and invited Frances to join them to see the exciting new country. Adventure appealed to Frances. She came along for the ride — and a rough ride it was.

Bishop Bumpas thought the northwest was literally God's country, an assurance of the continued affection of a benevolent providence for the human race. Frances couldn't share the bishop's enthusiasm. It seemed to her a dreary waste of muskeg, mosquitos, and Indians, and most of the time there were no Indians. The only thing she found to interest her was Henry Barrington Round, clerk of the Hudson's Bay post in Fort Hay River. Before Bishop Bumpas returned to England, he married them.

Hay River in the 1870s offered no life for a Victorian gentlewoman. There was not a candle to read by, or sew by, or paint by. And no fur to keep warm by, since every scrap of fur belonged to Henry's employers.

In 1887, he lost his job in a miscarriage of justice which roused indignation then and for years afterwards. He was running the post at Dunvegan. The company sent up a herd of cows. Henry found that one of the cows had tuberculosis and shot it. Half a year later, when the Company found what he had done, he was fired. He was told he should have got authority from Winnipeg. He protested that it would have taken six months and by that time all the cows would be dead. The Company didn't dispute the merit of his argument, but rules were rules and he was fired anyway.

The Rounds were plunged into years of mind-numbing hardship. Stranded on the frontier, unable to return to England, they stayed on in Edmonton, and Henry ground out a wretched living packing furs for McDougall and Secord, the free traders. The settlement could offer no occupation suitable to a Victorian gentleman, and Henry and Frances were in their sixties before the civilization they represented finally caught up to them and Henry could spend his closing years dealing in such a civilized product as Glenora, a place with the lieutenant-governor as a neighbour and the Carruthers Caveat as protection against shacks.

The caveat, dated December 2, 1911, has been modified to allow a school, but no store intrudes and the minimum cost of a house remains inviolate. If you build in Glenora, your house can't cost less than three thousand dollars.

32

The

Tomato

Case

The Tomato Case defined the personal and judicial temper of Barnsley Hughes, police magistrate in Edmonton from 1912 to 1928.

Barnsley Hughes was a gentleman of the old school — or out of an old book penned by Charles Dickens. He had already logged fifty-seven years when he appeared here from Tunbridge Wells, England, in 1910. And while he adopted his country with pioneer zest, he couldn't quite adjust to new ideas on clothing and continued to patronize his old tailor, who, from far-off Tunbridge Wells, kept him in old-fashioned coats with old-fashioned capes, in which he liked to take old-fashioned walks, swinging an old-fashioned cane, in a manner so agreeable that people he met couldn't withhold a pleasant word of greeting. This he would acknowledge with a gravely genial smile, which would be maintained if he happened to meet them in his court.

Unlike our senior magistrate of the time, Colonel P.C.H. Primrose, he had not a lifetime experience in law enforcement. Unlike our lady magistrate, Mrs. Emily Murphy, he was not a reformer. He was an architect and engineer, and his first interest here was the McMurray oilsands. At age sixty, he and his son Percy set off to explore and stake claims in the sands. It was winter. The railroad went only to Athabasca Landing. From there, the journey was on the frozen Athabasca by dog team. On the return, he made the ninety miles to Edmonton on a railroad handcar with the fresh-air top, a feat of remarkable endurance for a man who had spent most of a full life in the tranquil comfort of Tunbridge Wells. But Barnsley Hughes dismissed the hardships with a genial shrug.

In 1912, he took his geniality to the magistrate's chair, where his view of the law and its application tended to be good news for defendants.

The geniality extended through the hours of night and was often put to some strain. Police procedure was more cumbersome in his time. Nowadays, if "ye git a little drunk and ye land in jail," you can bail yourself out by paying the desk sergeant. But in the tenure of Barnsley Hughes, only a magistrate could swing wide the prison gates. When prominent citizens were hauled in for celebrating to excess, they would, upon recovering some of their senses, send for Barnsley to let them out.

They wouldn't dare wake the forbidding Magistrate Primrose at two o'clock in the morning, nor would they think of rooting Mrs. Murphy, a crusading prohibitionist, out of bed. But good old Barnsley was a sport. He'd come down. And he did. But he'd take his time about it and appear dressed as for a Sunday promenade.

The procedure on warrants was equally cumbersome. When Edmonton's finest had a warrant needing a magistrate's signature, discretion forbade their disturbing Colonel Primrose at three a.m.; gallantry forbade their waking Mrs. Murphy. But good old Barnsley was a sport. He'd sign.

They'd bang on the door of his house, just behind the Hecla Block off 95 Street. Barnsley would put on his Tunbridge Wells dressing gown, come to his desk, and sign the warrant with grave geniality. And if, as often happened, the rascal for whom the warrant was intended should appear before him in court a few hours later, the disturbance would not be held against him.

The kindly magistrate was especially understanding toward citizens who appeared before him charged with offences involving the flowing bowl. Many a bleary and head-sick man, sure that his life could never again be beautiful, got his first urge to try again when he found the gravely twinkling eyes of Barnsley Hughes fixed upon him.

Liquor offences had a long tradition in the courts, but in the tenure of Barnsley Hughes, engineering science presented a new set of problems embodied in the motor car. Barnsley ran our first traffic court with no centuries of legal precedent to guide him. Drivers of motor cars daily devised new and novel ways to collide with each other, with pedestrians, with fixed objects. Magistrate Hughes had to improvise rules of thumb to keep pace with the drivers.

While coping with the hottest new mode of transportation, Barnsley demonstrated to a large audience that he could still cope with an old one. A team of horses made a runaway bolt down Jasper Avenue. While other onlookers stood helpless or scattered, Barnsley took command. Unhurried as ever, he calmly planted himself on the route of the panic-stricken horses. At the precise moment, he grasped the hitching apparatus in the precise place and brought the incident to a harmless halt.

This show-stopping performance by a gentleman of seventy earned the applause of the multitude, which the hero dismissed with a slow smile. It showed that the man with the goatee and quaint clothes trod the streets of Edmonton with unhurried dignity because he chose to — not because he had to.

Barnsley Hughes cleared his last docket days before his death in 1928, displaying to the end the approach to law and its application which produced his most famous judgement — in a proceeding known as the Tomato Case.

Accused was a storekeeper, charged with selling a can of tomatoes on Wednesday afternoon, in contravention of the city's early-closing bylaw. The storekeeper was caught with the goods — canned. However, Barnsley Hughes dismissed the Tomato Case with a judgement of Solomon:

"The bylaw states that it is permissible to sell perishable goods on a Wednesday afternoon. Tomatoes in their natural state are certainly perishable. I am not prepared to state that tomatoes are no longer perishable when put in a tin."

That was justice tempered with Barnsley.

33

The
Dominion
Cigar Store

When Edmonton was young, a man's cigar was part of his costume — as much as his Christie stiff or his celluloid collar or his spats or his Cadillac, if he was in the real estate business, which, if he was a real live-wire, he probably was.

A man's cigar could tell you a good deal about him, and a man was supposed to smoke a cigar. Grandfather Gorman did, and classed the man who puffed cigarettes with the man who wore a wristwatch or patent leather shoes or carried his handkerchief in his sleeve — which is to say, if he was a man at all, he wasn't much of one.

Grandfather Gorman was often in a minority with his opinions but not in this case, which made the Dominion Cigar Store a hub of early Edmonton, right from 1911 when it opened on the northwest corner of First and Jasper. And if a gentleman who smoked cigarettes was no man, a woman who did was no lady, deemed a member of a social class frowned upon by church and state. A lady who lighted up in the lobby of the Macdonald Hotel on opening night 1915 was shown the door.

Harry V. Shaw cigar factory — one of three in Edmonton.
Photo courtesy of the City of Edmonton Archives EB 26-41; used by permission.

Joe Lauerman's Dominion Cigar Store was not by any means the only one in town. At 100 Street, two other Joes ran an impressive shop complete with fifteen barber chairs — Joe Dechene, who was later Member of Parliament for the eastern Alberta district of St. Paul later to 1957, and Joe McNeil, who, name notwithstanding, was as French-Canadian as Dechene and later sold cigars at 104 Street.

The Dominion was not the only store, but it had pride of location, a hub in its own right on Edmonton's traffic hub, in the hubbub of newsboys chanting the excellence of the *Journal*, *Bulletin*, or *Capital*, teamsters cussing motorists and each other, streetcars on their daily grind. Tom Adams and Sam Kennedy, the policemen controlling traffic, could see and hear it all from the centre of the crossing, and were bound to observe real estate operators detach themselves from the throng to enter the Dominion Cigar Store, there to solemnize a deal with Major

Cigars in action at the Dominion Cigar Store.
Photo courtesy of the City of Edmonton Archives EA 26-419; used by permission.

Reno cigars. The dark, thick Major Reno, commemorating the American civil war hero and western swashbuckler who gave his name to Reno, Nevada, was the official cigar of the real estate boom.

A man in a blindfold would know he was in the Dominion Cigar Store: his nose would tell him. Today all stores smell the same — much character has been sacrificed to plastic packaging. But the Dominion exuded the oily essence of cured tobacco, smoky even before being lit.

Add to that the clean smell of fresh cedar. Cigars came in cedar boxes with hinged lids and were recycled as catch-alls for household storage. In the dim light of the store they glowed with cigar-box art — nineteenth-century generals and Egyptian temptresses in rich, oily ivories, reds, greens, and golds. Fumed oak glowed in the dark, varnished until it wouldn't support another drop. Mahogany display cases were varnished till they gleamed ripe cherry. The big cedar cabinet with the drawers glowed with brass fittings. Each drawer was a humidor for special customers, each with its own key, and Joe Lauerman's staff kept them stocked to the patron's taste. From below, floor tiles radiated Byzantine patterns. From above, light was strained through cut glass. All around, mirrors of monumentally heavy plate magnified the scene of varnished splendour, appropriate to the cigar ceremony, cousin to the tea ceremony of the mysterious East. If the bank was a temple of commerce in 1911, the cigar store was a chapel.

Seventeen- and eighteen-year-olds, making claim on the estate of man, liked to break in on Peg-Tops, which sold for a nickel and had a wooden plug at one end, which pulled out so the smoker didn't have to bite through to create a draft. There were Book and Clay Small Cigars. Dark, oily Preferentias from Cuba. Otaras from the West Indies. The Davis Nobleman.

These were imports and popular, but the demand for local products was so brisk that Edmonton supported three cigar factories here and one in Stettler, which sent the popular Van Loo and pioneered keeping cigars fresh by packing them in tins. In Edmonton, E.B. Olsen produced the Nile Queen in a factory up First Street. Harry Shaw turned out the popular La Palma at two for a quarter and the Major Reno, official cigar of the boom, at three for fifty cents. The Major Reno also separated the men from the boys. Anyone who could hack it belonged with the real men — like Billy McNamara, mayor in 1914, who closed every deal with a Major Reno.

Even in the heyday of the cigar there was a group, mainly blue-collar, who held that real men didn't smoke tobacco but chewed it. And the chewers were reason enough for the store to be open at seven a.m.

It was open to midnight for the cigar trade, but the gentlemen who held that true manhood lay in chewing and spitting the stuff liked to pick up a plug on their way to a day's work, and the Dominion Cigar Store was at their service.

The favourite of the spittoon trade was the Prince of Wales plug, and while there might appear to be little in the Prince of Wales plug to interest the Canada Council, let there be no well-bred sneers. McGill University was built on it.

It sold mightily early in the day. When real estate operators appeared on the streets with their roller maps, the accent was on cigars. And there was a flurry of activity after dinner when the boys stopped in to check their humidors and pick up their supply before heading out for an evening of fun and games. At the Northern Club ... or the Dominion Club ... or the long bar of the Alberta Hotel ... or Monte Carlo's restaurant ... or the Elite Pool Room ... or the Elks Club ... or the King Edward Hotel ... or Lewis Brothers' Café ... or ...

34

The First Alberta Marathon

The First Alberta Marathon, widely advertised as such, ran on Victoria Day 1908 from the Alberta Hotel in downtown Edmonton to the fair grounds at Fort Saskatchewan, although the route totalled only 19 miles, 234 yards because the pioneer district could not muster a passable road of the regulation 26 miles, 385 yards.

The marathon was more than the premier attraction in a sports day program including paper chases for the young, horse races, soccer, lacrosse, baseball — pitting the Edmonton Young Liberals against the Vegreville Fire Eaters — and a concert by the Fort Saskatchewan Fire Brigade Band, a program so dazzling it prompted 2,710 Edmontonians to pay the Canadian Northern Railway 55 cents a head to board excursion trains. Above and beyond all that, it was the Alberta trial for the Olympic Games.

The fourth Olympiad of the modern era was to be held in England that summer, the marathon route to be from Windsor Castle to White City Stadium in London. Only eighteen countries were participating —

the Canadian Olympic Association was recognized in 1907, tenth in rank among the 199 of today — so there was no real limit to the number of runners a country could enter. The winner of the Alberta Trial would be entitled to line up with the starters in the royal gardens at Windsor.

As the big day drew near, Jackson Brothers, the jewellers, proudly advertised that they were designing and manufacturing the trophies for the marathon, including a gold medal worth a hundred dollars for the winner.

On Saturday, May 23, contestants were to register at the Edmonton Young Liberals Club. Fifteen put in their names and drew numbers, but by Monday morning seven had apparently remembered previous engagements and failed to answer the nine o'clock starting gun fired by Frank Walker. Frank represented Fort Saskatchewan in the first Alberta legislature and had wrangled this important Olympic trial away from Calgary.

From the hotel at 98 Street and Jasper, the contestants broke for 96 Street (Kinistino Avenue), then pounded north along the wooden side- walk to the city limit — Rat Creek at 110 Avenue.

Across the creek, the Fort Trail began among the houses of dubious diversion in Norwood. With recent rains, the trail was muddy and heavy as far as the packing plant in North Edmonton. But from there on it was sandy and actually improved by rain.

Art Burn of Calgary was favoured because of his experience and training, and shot to the lead as the runners turned up 96 Street. Art had been racing for seven years. He had won some prestigious events, including the Boston Five Mile, and his trainer was the legendary Jimmy McEwan, whose clients numbered Billy Lauder, Canadian lightweight boxing champion, and the Caledonian soccer club of Calgary, also national champions.

Art was sponsored by the Calgary Athletic Association, whose mem- bers were betting heavily on him. They were taking bets from the Edmonton Young Liberals, sponsors of Billy Turner and Tommy Evans; from backers of Bill Lyons, the tinsmith; F.W. Moon of Strathcona; Gilbert Johnson of Innisfail; Fred Fraser of Fort Chipewyan; and Albert McIntyre. Albert was a grain buyer in Strathcona, and his prowess as a sprinter gave him a business edge. When a grain wagon drove in sight of Saskatchewan Drive, he could outrace his competitors to enter the first bid.

Along the trail, officials on haystacks and similar points of vantage kept field glasses trained on the action to ensure the athletes were neither hindered nor helped contrary to the Olympic ideal. And there was apparently no Olympic rule against a friend on horseback trotting alongside a runner to shield him from the pesky crosswind. Two officials rode behind the pack in the automobile of Charlie May, the postmaster, and they offered no objection to the outriders flanking Art Burn and Fred Fraser.

The Canadian Northern Railway joined in the fun, with a special train providing vantage viewpoints to those betting on the race. Where the railroad track crossed the wagon track, the train stopped, the runners panted by, and bets might be increased. From the last viewpoint the special barrelled full-steam to the Fort so the bettors could be in at the finish.

Six thousand throats saluted Art Burn as he entered the fair ground and cruised past the finish line two hours plus forty-five seconds from the Alberta Hotel. Art was then off to the Olympics where he enjoyed one mile of glory.

At the first milepost out of Windsor Castle, he was second among the eighty runners, although most passed him on the road to White City.

But at the Olympic trial that ended in Fort Saskatchewan, the cheers were just as mighty for the man who was second at the finish line, six minutes and fifty seconds after Burn.

Fred Fraser was what racing in pioneer Alberta was all about. Sporting investors were always hoping to spot a challenger coming out of the woods, an unknown they could back with wagers against the reigning champion.

Fred Fraser was literally out of the woods, on holiday from Fort Chipewyan, where he mushed dog teams along the snowy trails of the north. A rangy, limber twenty-three-year old, Fred was a grandson of Colin Fraser, the fabled Scots piper whose blazing pipes had heralded the approach of Sir George Simpson on tours of the Hudson's Bay

Company empire. Fred's emergence as competition for Art Burn was reported by the *Edmonton Bulletin* on May 21:

He was discovered only the other day by several enthusiasts and in order to be sure that he was really the pure goods they tried him out on the road. Fred did the run from the Fort to Edmonton on a record that made the eyes of the sports bulge. Nothing will now satisfy Fred's backers until they see him in the race on Monday.

Fred ran in his workday moccasins and provided a good day's work for his backers. What they lost at excellent odds to Burn supporters, they more then recouped on those who came after Fred.

The *Bulletin* was entranced by Fred's potential: "With hard training and good living he should show up well in another year among the long distance runners of Canada." Whatever the paper meant by good living, hard training meant he'd have to change his running style — "lifting himself too much and wasting his strength."

But that was the style of the dog-team driver, developed through generations to ease the way over snowbound trails. Fred needed it in his business and couldn't pursue the suggested route to national recognition.

But in winters that lay ahead, on solitary runs through silent woods, he would hear the cheers of the crowd at the First Alberta Marathon.

35

Selkirk

Days

From 1901 until fire brought it down in 1963, the Selkirk Hotel (née the Windsor) anchored the southwest corner of First and Jasper.

The hotel lobby was on the second of its three storeys and led out to a balcony that overlooked both streets. Madelaine Carroll played a balcony scene there in World War Two, selling Victory Bonds to a rally that blocked traffic.

The blonde British actress is one of many personalities linked with the Selkirk, a group in which the keynote personality was Bob McDonald.

Bob arrived on the scene in 1901, after a poverty-driven boyhood in Cape Breton and a rugged young manhood in the mountains of B.C. Obtaining a lowly job in the hotel, he soon owned it, along with the Yale, east along Jasper.

But two hotels were not enough to absorb all his zest. He had a string of trotting horses. He had a string of fighters. He had a baseball club. He had the first Stanley Steamer in Edmonton, and in an age when automobiles went pop-pop-pop-pop-pop-pop-pop, Bob rolled along the avenues in a vehicle that went *shweeeee ... shweeeee*. When Bob's unfailing business instinct told him the Stanley Steamer would never be universal, he got the agency for Studebakers and sold Studebaker taxis to his long-time tenant in the Selkirk, Jack Hays.

When Bob bought the hotel, he had a sign painter make him a sign to advise passersby that SPIRITUOUS AND FERMENTED LIQUORS were available in the bar. The signsmith was long on art but short on spelling and delivered a board proclaiming SPIRITUOUS AND FRE-MENTED LIQUORS. Bob thought it was a good joke and left the sign up for years. A further invitation shone from the roof of the hotel — perhaps the first moving electrical sign in town. Naked white light bulbs outlined the shape of a pudgy, contented bear. Other lights outlined the source of his contentment, a bottle of beer from the Edmonton Brewing and Malting Co. Ltd. Still other bulbs went off and on to show Papa Bear lifting the bottle to his grateful lips — a reminder that this fine Edmonton product was available in the Selkirk bar, along with spiri-tuous and "fremented" liquors. And there was more in the bar. That's where Bob kept his fighters.

In the boomtime that preceded the first world war, Bob promoted fights at the Thistle Rink and the Opera House on Third Street. When his fighters weren't fighting, he gave them gainful employment dishing up suds. It was good for business and saved the expenses of bouncers. No need for such a specialist when he had Louis "Kid" Scaler, the western welterweight champion, tending bar. Or "Fighting Dick" Hyland, who had gone with Ad Wolgast and Battling Nelson.

Bob had a soft spot for old boxers down on their luck, which accounted for Bill Burns, the grouchy old cuss who sold papers in front of the Selkirk and was a non-paying guest of the hotel. People used to wonder why, but Bob figured boxing owed a debt to men like Bill Burns and he intended to pay it.

Bill was a relic of the bad old days of prizefighting when it was illegal in most American states. Bob heard repeatedly about the time Bill fought on a barge, on a river between two states. The promoter had arranged for the police to raid the affair as soon as the fight ended. The fans took off through the woods in all directions. The promoter took off too — with the money. Stories like this brought about the Edmonton Boxing and Wrestling Commission.

Overhead view, looking west on Jasper towards the original First Presbyterian Church, at 103 Street. Photo courtesy of the author.

In 1913, Bob and his pal Dr. J.P. McCormack — and their mutual pal Alderman Joe Driscoll, the Sportsman's Candidate — saw the commission set up.

Bob had an office of course, but he preferred a seat on the top step of the stairway that came up to the lobby. He liked to sit there swapping greetings with the patrons, or swapping yarns with pals like his brother Jim, who ran the Yale Hotel; or Jack Calhoun, who owned the King Edward; or Abe Cristall, who owned the Royal George; or Richard Secord. In wealthy old age, pioneer trader Secord became a connoisseur of fine wines and on afternoons not fit to work liked to drop up with a bottle of some pleasing vintage and sit on the top step swapping stories and the bottle. Talk ranged far and wide, but inevitably included boxing and yarns about a bartender who had worked for Bob before the first world war.

Jack McKernan was the smallest bartender, weighing in at no better than 130 pounds after Christmas dinner, but he could still handle bouncer's duties. He was a student of boxing, a practising fighter, coach, and manager. He was a sharp dresser, perhaps a trifle too sharp, and was sharpest when cards were on the table. He was also the gabbiest bartender in town.

By tradition a man who ministered to the thirsty was a listener — speaking only for wise counsel. But Jack McKernan never stopped talking. He did not talk so fast, really, but with an intensity that defied interruption. Here is a sample of McKernan recalled by a customer who stood across the polished oak slab from him:

So I say to this guy throw the left. But does he throw the left? No, he don't throw the left. So I say to him — how come you don't throw the left? And he says to me — why should I throw the left? So I say to him — look, Mac, it's to me a matter of no consequence if you throw the left or you DON'T throw the left, but as a disinterested observer, were I in your predicament I would throw the left.

When war came in 1914, boxing slowed down, and when prohibition came two years later, bartending stopped altogether. Bob McDonald converted the Selkirk bar to Johnson's Café; Jack McKernan drifted back to his native Oakland, California, looking for a new angle.

Naturally, he looked for one in the prize ring, and his quick eye recognized opportunity in a twenty-two-year-old heavyweight who was not impressing anyone else. The newspapers had given up on him. Three managers had given up on him. He gave up on himself and went to Seattle and got a job in the shipyards.

When Bob's bartender discovered where the disheartened young man had taken himself, he sent telegrams offering to line up some bouts. He sent three, which his prospect was too discouraged to answer. So McKernan went to Seattle in person and urged the young fellow to take some advice. He should forget about boxing technique. All he had to do was pull up his socks and knock those bums over — and he could be heavyweight champion of the world.

In eighteen months, McKernan's judgement proved correct. And if you're any student of the manly art of self-defence, you'll have recognized the disillusioned fighter Bob McDonald and his pals discussed at the top of the stairs as Jack Dempsey — and bartender Jack McKernan of the Selkirk Hotel as Jack Kearns.

36

Ross
Hall

The sign over the building in Old Strathcona reads W.E. ROSS 1894 —
which is correct as far as it goes, but there's more to the story.

Will Ross had the first hardware store on Whyte Avenue. One of the
sages of Old Strathcona, Colonel Fred Jamieson, explained that he was
called Will because people liked him. If they hadn't, he'd have been Ross.
If they were neither for him nor against him, he'd have been Bill. But
since they liked him so much, they called him Will.

Will was born in a Scottish shire with so many Rosses it was known
officially as Rossshire. Will's family included eight brothers and a sister,
so many Rosses that the family moved to Nova Scotia. By 1891, Will was
married and had eleven little Rosses of his own, enough to stock a
western town. He'd done well in business and decided to scout
prospects for young Rosses in the Canadian northwest.

The train brought him to the end of the railroad in the centre of the
phenomenon now known as Old Strathcona. He arrived towards the
end of the beautiful summer that inspired Thomas G. Pearce to mint the
slogan "Sunny Alberta."

Through the beautiful winter of 1891–92, when men worked in the
open without gloves, he went about setting up a business and building a

home for his family, who arrived in time for the fearful winter of 1892–93. Eventually there were three more little Rosses, for a total of fourteen. Will had Gaelic pet names for them all, having never lost his native language; Isabel, the youngest, was Ishbel Vec, *vec* meaning small. And his greeting for all comers was *cia mar a tha thu an diugh*, Gaelic for "how are you today?".

The Rosses were a musical family. Will loved the old Scottish tunes like "Nut Brown Maiden," which he often sang in a warm Highland baritone; but as a founder of Knox Presbyterian Church, he couldn't allow the piano to be played on the Sabbath except for hymns. So he got around the Sabbath by promoting "Nut Brown Maiden" and other old favourites to hymns. Music ran deep through the clan. Will's grand-nephew Robert Preston won fame on Broadway as the Music Man, and further renown in the classic Hollywood film.

In 1894, Will's monument went up on Whyte Avenue. The hardware store on the ground floor was a significant contribution to community life, but the hall upstairs was something greater.

Ross Hall was to Old Strathcona what Robertson's Hall was to Edmonton. Both were upstairs; both were centres for events social, cultural, and political. But Robertson's burned down in 1906, while Ross' survives to this day, with its memories of nights when lights stayed on late.

Dances put the building to a structural test. People literally danced all night, especially to the tunes of Larry Garneau and his tireless fiddle.

Many occasions were informal, but some were "swell" affairs to which "Piggy" Smith would come in faultless evening dress cut for him by his London tailor. "Piggy" was an English eccentric who preferred the company of porkers on a steady basis and worked on a pig farm in Bonnie Doon, but whenever a "swell" affair beckoned, he brought a touch of Savile Row to Ross Hall.

One such affair was the stuff of legend. The Mounted Police were coming from Fort Saskatchewan, splendid in their scarlet tunics. The tunics were indeed splendid, but the riders of the plains didn't realize they weren't supposed to wear spurs to a formal dance. The spurs carved many a niche in "swell" gowns.

On other nights, the hall became a theatre for local drama groups and touring stock companies playing the backwoods with comedies like *Mr. Plaster of Paris* — a real knee-slapper that.

On some nights, the stage became a speaker's platform for rallies both political and civic. Women didn't have a vote, but members of the Women's Christian Temperance Union would take front-row seats, the better to poll candidates for their views on the demon rum. Sir Frederick Haultain, last premier of the Northwest Territories, spoke there. So did Whyte Avenue lawyer A.C. Rutherford, first premier of Alberta. A future prime minister of Canada, Calgary lawyer R.B. Bennett, brought his style of oratory to Ross Hall. Another Calgary lawyer, Paddy Nolan, brought the style which won him a gold medal for oratory in his Dublin days. The titled founder of the Cochrane ranch, and godfather of the town, brought his vision of the British Empire on the prairies.

Ross Hall was witness to stirring events in 1899 as the community moved towards incorporation. Since the arrival of the railroad — and Will Ross — in 1891, it had been a vigorous entity, growing to a population of 1600, but with no official status or official name. The sign on the station read *Edmonton*, a hint by the railroad that the real Edmonton lay not across the river but on the south side. The Strathcona Hotel was the *Edmonton House*. The post office was designated *Edmonton South*. Hardly appropriate for a go-ahead settlement determined to outgrow and outshine the tired fur-trading post on the north bank. A proper name was in order, but that wasn't the main reason for incorporation.

Colonel Jamieson said it was for the same reason the United Way incorporated — because of the multiplicity of appeals. And he'd be a hard man to refute. A precise, soft-spoken soldier and lawyer who observed events while training for the law in the office of Premier Rutherford, his knowledge was so great you could have clapped a set of book covers on him and proclaimed him an encyclopedia of Strathcona.

A hat was always being passed for some community improvement. The process might start with W.H. Sheppard, the hotel man. On deciding there should be a new sidewalk somewhere, he'd write a note, attach a ten-dollar bill, and pass it on. Ochsner the brewer might attach a five-dollar bill. Harry Wilson the postmaster might add five. In his law office, A.C. Rutherford might add ten. In the hardware store, Will Ross might add five. It would come to Jim McKernan, the hotel man, who used to joke that he was always being asked to support Atlantic events on Pacific holidays — his code for athletic events on civic holidays. Jim would attach ten, and there would be enough to hire a man to build the wooden sidewalk. Then the next week someone would decide that a new horse trough would add to the metropolitan amenities of Whyte Avenue and around would go the hat again.

Hat passing gave the community reach beyond the narrow surveyed limits. Road-cutting projects went into the woods and into the south side. Whyte Avenue was extended three miles to connect with the Clover Bar road allowances. To the west, a winter road beckoned German settlers from Stony Plain. They had to come south to get around the swamp of Jasper Place anyway, and the road led to a crossing on the ice at Whitemud Creek.

Not all volunteer improvements had a commercial inspiration. While the rival town over the river was busy walling off its valley view, residents along Saskatchewan Drive were keeping it open for future generations. They cleaned out the bank across from their property, plowed it up, rolled it out and put it into grass, and after a century it's "greener" than ever.

Passing the hat brought progress officially organized communities would envy, but the multiplicity of appeals was a burden and cheapskates were annoying. They could enjoy the view and the sidewalk and the horse trough without contributing.

Ross Hall was the site of the civic gathering to choose a name for the soon-to-be-incorporated village. New Omaha took the early lead. A group of settlers from Nebraska thought that would send a message of a place bound for greatness. Someone suggested Minto, for a former governor general. A wag raised a laugh proposing McCauleyville, for Matt McCauley, the first mayor of Edmonton. But the choice was Strathcona. Lord Strathcona was high in the councils of the CPR, which, through a subsidiary, owned half the building lots in town. The main thoroughfare was already named for Sir William Whyte, another big man in the CPR.

So Strathcona it was, and later that year a crowd in Ross Hall cheered Thomas Bennett, the first mayor, when he stood on the platform to make his famous predictions about the effect incorporation would have on the rival town over the river. To ringing rafters he declared: "Grass will grow in the streets of Edmonton!"

Another slice of history filed under the heading W.E. ROSS 1894.

37

Ford

Theatre

When Dr. John Darley Harrison first gazed on Edmonton in 1892, he had to fight the river. In fur trade time, the river was man's friend, showing him the way through the wilderness, floating his pelts down to market. But with the appearance of trails and railroads, the river suddenly became a barrier, a nuisance to be crossed, tolerated only for its utility in water and sewer systems.

Dr. Harrison was impatient to get to Edmonton and begin his practice of medicine. He'd come all the way from Montreal with his medical books and instruments and was in a hurry because he had come west to die. Of tuberculosis.

In summer, he would have crossed on John Walter's ferry; in winter, he could cross on ice. But when he and the driver of the horse-drawn hack gazed on the river, it wasn't quite winter and wasn't quite spring. The ice was clearly the stuff on which angels fear to tread, but he knew if he didn't get across then, he'd be stranded on the south bank till the ice broke up and drifted off with the current. In the interval, only mail and express parcels could cross, pulled along the ferry cable.

So he and the driver decided to make a dash for it. They put on an exciting race with the crumbling ice but lost, leaving the doctor standing in waist-deep water while his books and supplies were swept away, all but a vial of chloroform in his vest pocket. Scrambled ashore, he had little time to weigh his loss or the wetness and misery of his condition because someone else was worse off. A blacksmith at Fort Edmonton had suffered a skull fracture and broken bones were pressing on his brain.

In the blacksmith's forge, the doctor converted an iron nail to a surgical hook. With the chloroform saved in his vest pocket, he operated to relieve the pressure.

The patient survived. So did Dr. Harrison, for forty-six years, his tuberculosis cured by Alberta air.

It was fortunate that he'd raced the ice at the Ford, so that even in defeat he could wade ashore, safely if ingloriously. Before bridges, before ferries, freight crossed the river at the Ford. Until dams upstream stabilized the river's flow, the Ford would come into view in the fall. Pedestrians taking the autumn air on the east walk of the High Level Bridge would look down on a gravel bar creeping out from the north bank towards another emerging from the south. Sometimes they would see kids claiming kinship with the great adventurers by wading the channel through water thirty inches deep.

John Walter's ferry was just downstream from the Ford and it was an environmentalist's dream, moving entirely on the power of the current. Saturday night revellers liked to rent the ferry, anchor it in midstream, and hear their songs echo from the cliffs. The ferry was once the object of a dramatic chase. A lumberjack came hurtling out of the woods just as the ferry left the south bank, imploring Johnny McFadden to come back for him. That wasn't possible, so the woodsman dived in and came swimming in pursuit. He caught up easily and then had a second thought. He swam the rest of the way, beat the ferry to the landing, and saved his five cents for entertainment.

There may have been comedy at the ferry, but at the Ford there was drama. A herd of horses made dramatic excitement for men shouting in the water and those calling encouragement from the banks. And even a few head of cattle made a splash of importance to the Edmonton district.

Two famous dramas involved heavy implements. One was a piano, which attempted the crossing in 1883. It weighed six hundred pounds, as a full-size upright should, and came from the factory of Knabe and

Company in Baltimore. It had come most recently from Seaforth, Ontario, with the family effects of Scott Robertson. It had survived the rails to Calgary and the trail ride north, but if it failed at the Ford, all that would go for nought.

Being upright and standing tall were traits admired in pioneer country, but for a piano on a wagon in a river ford, standing tall raised the centre of gravity and the danger of a disastrous tip. In late October, the river was at its lowest and slowest but still presented a nerve-wracking challenge. Suspense was electric among Robertson and other watchers on the banks. Groans and gasps as the Knabe tipped this way. Relief as it became an upright piano again. Gasps and groans as it tipped that way. If it capsized, it would not survive to become the first piano in Edmonton. The year previous the Long family had brought a spinet across for their home at Namao, but this was the first full-size piano.

Fortunately, it survived the crossing.

In the fall of 1895, a crowd gathered to watch another large implement challenge the Ford. A steam traction engine was to make the attempt — on its own power. These hissing monsters came up a third the size of a railroad locomotive and rumbled around pioneer country on their own steam, bringing power to harvest grain crops and forests. At four to five miles per hour, they hissed from farm to logging camp to farm, steaming on anything that would burn — wood, coal, peat, hay, straw, mail-order catalogues. Atop each monster hung a giant drive wheel. At a farm or lumber camp, steam was switched from locomotion to the big wheel, which then drove a belt connected to threshing machine or rotary saw. So important were they to the pioneer economy that the highway policy of the first government of Alberta set a standard for bridges — sturdy enough to take a steam traction engine.

The audience, gathered along the banks as fans on opposite sides of a stadium, knew the importance of the drama as well as they knew the star. Frank Walker was the driver. At twenty-four, Frank was a popular figure in the community, a young man destined for drama. In Edmonton's original Klondike Days, Frank would be one of the handful of adventurers hardy enough to travel to the goldfields by the overland trail, surviving, en route, a winter on the Liard River. And when Alberta elected its first legislature, the body which framed the policy on bridges and steam engines, Frank would be among the chosen twenty-five.

The crowd knew how eagerly the monster was awaited at farms and lumber camps to the north. Crops were at stake. So was the investment of Frank's brother, who owned the monster. It was the heaviest, most powerful contraption around. If it capsized, or the river got into the firebox and snuffed the steam, there was no other contraption to pull it from an ignominious grave.

The drama was no one-man show. Frank entered the current with a large supporting cast. A convoy of men on horseback and men in boats churned the waters, sounding the mysteries of the river bottom. The drama was in many acts, all the same. The convoy would crowd around in consultation. Frank would send up a puff of steam and the monster would edge a few yards onwards. Surge by surge — bet by bet — it gained the north bank and emerged dripping but with its firebox high and dry.

Then it was off, coming to the aid of the party with a crop to thresh or logs to saw. For drama, no theatre could compete with the Ford.

38

Socialist Legislation

It was a narrow escape. You could read all about it — as the newsboys chanted — in the *Edmonton Bulletin* of May 7, 1906: CITY COUNCIL ADOPTS RADICAL AMENDMENT TO CITY CHARTER BUT TAKES IT BACK ON CONSIDERATION.

The escape was engineered by the oratory of Alderman John R. Boyle. Our charter as a city had been issued in 1904 by the Northwest Territories. Councillors were asking the new legislature of the new province of Alberta to upgrade the charter in various ways so Edmonton could meet its new responsibilities as provincial capital.

Radicals on council saw a greater role for women. They proposed extending to women the same voting rights enjoyed by men. Voting was not enjoyed by all men — only those twenty-one or over owning five hundred dollars' worth of property. Alderman Ralph Bellamy wanted to extend those rights to women on the same basis, but the city solicitor argued that it wasn't possible. Only single women and widows could be property owners — a married woman couldn't because her property was her husband's.

The prospect of ladies voting at provincial and federal levels was somewhere off in the future, but the municipal level would be a start.

Alderman Bellamy scaled down his motion and council voted to ask for the amendment by a vote of four to three.

Then came Alderman Boyle galloping to the rescue. They were asking the government for socialist legislation; it was sure to provoke large discussion in the house; if it were not taken out, all amendments might be sidetracked.

John R. Boyle's forecast of what the government might do was given considerable weight. In addition to being an alderman of the city, he was a member of the legislature, representing the riding of Sturgeon, and an important member, holding the post of deputy speaker. The town of Boyle, in his riding, would be named in his honour.

Mr. Boyle's ten minutes of warnings swayed only one alderman, but that was enough. Charlie May switched his vote from yea to nay, the nays squelched the idea four to three, and those who read all about it in the

Bulletin were advised that "Edmonton only escaped woman suffrage, and the possibility of a petticoat government last night, by Alderman May deciding to reconsider what he had done."

Although Edmonton may have breathed easier at the narrow escape, an irresistible force was in motion. Five years further on, the charter was amended without fuss to make polling an equal-opportunity event, and the tradition that a woman's property was her husband's had perished. This visibly impressed an American journalist who passed this way in 1911.

George Stephens described Edmonton as a pretty little town of thirty thousand, determined not to follow in the ruts left by older cities and aided in this ideal by its isolation, the nearest town of any consequence being Winnipeg. (Calgary papers please copy.) He predicted that Edmonton would soon be known as "Saint Edmonton," because citizens had nothing to swear at.

We had no "central" to swear at because of the automatic-dial telephone system, one of the first he'd seen; no piratical utilities barons to swear at because no private corporation owned the electric light and water meters; no bloated traction barons to swear at because the streetcar lines were owned by the citizens themselves; no tax system to swear at because a man was not penalized for building a good house — only the land was taxed. (That system, alas, was abandoned in 1918 and swearing has been in order ever since.) Of clinching importance for Mr. Stephens: there was nothing in the voting system to swear at. Men and women voted for councillors. All property owners, women included, had their say on money bylaws, and if a man hadn't acquired property but was smart enough to marry a woman who had, he could vote on the bylaw if he presented his wife's permission — in writing.

The irresistible force swept on. Another five years and the Alberta legislature came to a decision on admitting women to polling booths at the provincial level. Only one immovable object raised his voice to shout nay. And it wasn't the minister of education, the Honourable John R. Boyle.

39

It's in
the Mail

One day in 1923, Perren Baker, Alberta's minister of education, conferred in some agitation with his deputy, Fred McNally. Having just
returned from a tour of school districts, the minister outlined a
problem he'd found. He outlined a solution. Then he outlined a further
problem — the department had no money to pay for the solution.

Alberta education was literally a square deal. For purposes of
schooling, the province was organized in squares — four miles square,
or sixteen square miles the same thing, or sixty-four quarter sections,
each representing a family farm on which enterprising homesteaders
were converting the wilderness to agriculture. Within a square, families
were authorized to organize a school district, plant a one-room school
in the geometric centre, and hire a teacher. The system was working sur-
prisingly well, but north of Edmonton Mr. Baker had found a district so
poor the people couldn't afford any kind of school, and ten children
were growing up with no access to education.

As the minister responsible, he felt his department must do some
thing about it — the deprived kids must be sent regular lessons by mail.
And he offered a detailed description of the sort of person capable of

handling the task. This person must be a woman, a motherly sort of woman, a woman who had been a teacher, a linguist, a stenographer, and other qualifications which he would doubtless think of later.

Dr. McNally could think of one. This person must be able to create juvenile correspondence courses from scratch. Mail-order courses for adults were part of popular culture. Adults had learned bookkeeping, motor mechanics, and electronics through the mail. Ninety-seven-pound weaklings had been taught how to triumph over bullies in twenty-four body-building lessons delivered by the postman. But there was nothing available for the ten children without a school, forty miles north of Edmonton.

The successful candidate would also have a further qualification. She must be already on the frugal payroll of the department. Did such a person exist? The deputy minister called in Mrs. Sievewright.

Enter Elizabeth Sievewright, a small, vibrant package of clear-eyed energy and efficiency, unassuming modesty emphasized by a soft voice of the Highland shire of Inverness.

She had grown up among Scottish convictions about education, one of which was that it took as long to make a teacher as a doctor. After high school, a young man or woman aspiring to pedagogy underwent a three-year apprenticeship in classrooms, at the end of which he or she qualified for a provisional certificate and three years of Normal School — at the end of which he or she was urged to become a real teacher with three years' university.

For Elizabeth, marriage intervened after phase two, but she knew well the student life in Edinburgh University, among young Scots surviving on oatmeal, herring, and bread, sustained by a greater hunger for higher learning.

Like many Scots, her husband, a brilliant civil engineer named John Menzies, was fascinated by tales of Canada, and in 1907, he, Elizabeth, and their infant son arrived in Edmonton on a cross-country tour. They were only passing through, but John was persuaded to stay and work on the new domed legislature. And if they hadn't stayed, their son Dudley wouldn't have grown up to be public works commissioner for the city of Edmonton and have his name on the Dudley R. Menzies LRT bridge across the river. John had a relative here — Premier Rutherford — and had letters of introduction, but never presented them lest he might appear a favour-seeker. The premier only learned about his kinsman when John died of pneumonia in 1910.

Elizabeth tried "going home" to Scotland but quickly realized that Edmonton had become home and found a place for her talents in Alberta's fledging department of education. She married again, to Captain G.R. Sievewright of the auditor-general's department, and was widowed again when he died in France in 1916.

But she retained a calm conviction that things work out for the best. She lived on 71 Avenue, just off 109 Street, and twice every Sunday walked the two miles to Metropolitan Methodist Church to play the organ — weather always permitting, even in the worst of winter. Among her duties at the government, she counselled graduates of the normal schools, matching them with school boards in the country districts Perren Baker had been visiting. For all the above reasons, Fred McNally was sure he had the solution to the minister's problem when he called Mrs. Sievewright into his office on that day in 1923.

Often asked to recall that meeting, Mrs. Sievewright was compelled by modesty to say, "It was not my idea to start the correspondence branch." However, she was compelled by honesty to admit, " ... but I was the one chosen to start it."

By 2002, the program had grown into the Alberta Distance Learning Centre, with a budget of 12 million dollars, a staff of 108 (a third of them teachers), and 21,000 students, 80 percent at the high school level.

Mrs. Sievewright began at the Three Rs — and a one-on-one relationship with ten students, of whom there were fifty the next year and a thousand when she had to give up the work in 1936.

High-school courses were not added until 1939, but she couldn't abandon students who had completed the elementary grades by mail and came to Edmonton for matriculation. Their attitude reminded her too much of the students of her own youth who came to Edinburgh and lived on oatmeal and herring for the privilege of university. She collected money for them — and clothing to the extent that her basement often suggested a rummage sale in progress.

Her favourite was a boy from a Ukrainian settlement near St. Paul. He was an unattractive lad, physically awkward, even clumsier socially. But he had a burning thirst to learn — which in Mrs. Sievewright's Scottish view had to be saved.

She became his counsellor and coach. Often he had no socks. Once he had no shoes. He never had money, except for what she collected for him. But he lived on the equivalent of oatmeal and herring, and bulled his way through examinations because, if he failed, his father would make him come home. He passed out of grade twelve, got into university, and his personal finest hour arrived when his English and his poise advanced to the point where he could sing with the chorus in a student production of *HMS Pinafore* — and send Mrs. Sievewright a ticket.

He died overseas in the second world war, but something in him had been saved — something in him and hundreds of other youngsters beyond reach of regular schools.

At the end of a long life, Elizabeth Sievewright liked to be alone at times — to think about them, and the lad who sent her a ticket for *HMS Pinafore.*

40

Mike's
News
Stand

Mike's News Stand was on Jasper Avenue between 100 and 101 Street. Mike's was also where Edmonton was at — for half of the twentieth century.

The founder and chief executive spark of this institution was John Michaels, who, in 1912, began selling papers on the sidewalk at First and Jasper.

It was a far noisier corner then. The creaking of carts and shouts of teamsters. The clanging of streetcars grinding around the curve. The klaxon horns on Cadillacs of the real estate promoters. Incessant shouts of newsboys. Add above the tumult Mike bawling: "Get your home-town paper! Get your home-town paper!" Like Mike himself, most Edmontonians were newly arrived from someplace else, and the home-town paper was cherished reading.

Mike came from New York — lower east side, as his strident sales pitch indicated. He was twenty when he landed here in search of his pal Piggy Red O'Leary. From early boyhood, Mike and Red had hustled

First outdoor stand, about 1912. 101 Street and Jasper, northeast corner. John Michaels (left) with Bob Wright. Photo courtesy of the City of Edmonton Archives EA 10-1587; used by permission.

papers on the sidewalks of New York. Red had been found with tuber-culosis and had gone to northwest Canada to try to heal his lungs in fresh air on railroad construction gangs.

John Michaels landed in Edmonton broke, but in a few months of hustling papers had enough money to buy out Mickey Ryan and Walter Wolk. Their outdoor spot on the northwest corner of First and Jasper became the first Mike's News Stand, specializing in your home-town paper.

Whenever word reached Mike of a railroad work train coming into town, he'd be off to the depot looking for Red O'Leary. One day Red's train came in, and he and Mike were again share-alike partners as they'd been on the sidewalks of New York. Mike brought out two more pals from his home town and a fine Damon Runyon quartet they made —

ready to do a number in *Guys and Dolls* — Mike, Piggy Red O'Leary, Curly Shea, and Morris April.

The news stand couldn't use up all Mike's energy. The Arena (later the Gardens) opened for hockey on the exhibition grounds, and Mike was out there hustling. Edmonton had two hockey teams, the Eskimos and the Dominions, and Mike had just the thing for fans of both: "Pennants! Get your pennants!"

With the news stand a going concern, Mike soon branched out into wholesaling. He hustled around to Edmonton's three dailies — the *Bulletin*, the *Journal*, and the labour paper called the *Capital* — and hustled contracts to deliver papers to other news stands. With horse and buggy, he was away at top speed, tossing off bundles as he went. But the horse wasn't fast enough to suit Mike, and he soon acquired a four-wheeled vehicle with a motorcycle engine, a contraption in which he could make real time, up to six miles an hour. Unfortunately, the speed limit on the High Level Bridge was three, and Mike drew a speeding ticket. Next morning, he waited in court for his case to come up. Waited. And waited. Waiting was not Mike's game. Desperate, he asked the crown prosecutor when he'd be called. "Well, now, Mike, that's a strange thing. There was a man here named John Mitchell up for intoxication. When we called John Michaels, this Mitchell got up and pleaded guilty and paid your fine."

So Mike was off and running again, and soon had a motorcycle — with papers riding in the sidecar.

Within two years, Red O'Leary succumbed to TB. Curly Shea and Morris April heard the call of the canyons — of Manhattan skyscrapers — but Mike made his stand here. And in 1914 gave an intimation of the calibre of citizen Edmonton was gaining.

At twenty-two, he was the elder statesman of the street-sales gang and organized the Newsboys Band. In 1914, the newsboy was thought to be a lad whose daddy was in heaven — or in the corner saloon en route to the other place — and who sold papers to support his mother. Newsboys had a lot of time on their hands. To keep them out of trouble, Mike organized the band. He stirred up enthusiasm among the boys — he was good at that. He raised money to buy instruments — he was good at that. He made up the difference out of his own pocket — he was good at that. He didn't know anything about music, but he hired Sid Bullock to rehearse the band. They soon had a repertoire of three numbers and made their first public appearance in the summer of 1914, playing members of the Ad Club to the special train that would take them through middle America advertising Edmonton. Mike marched up Jasper Avenue at the head of the band, a sort of parade marshal and cheerleader, a preview of things to come.

When Sid Bullock went away with the army, Mike had to find another conductor. Women were coming forward to fill many positions, and Mike found Ruth Cutler, an Irish girl out from Boston with her family. *Abie's Irish Rose* was a popular play of the time, and Mike and Ruth played their own version. When Sid returned to take over the band, Ruth retired to other duties as Mrs. John Michaels.

December 5, 1916 is a date for the history file. On that day Mike's News Stand came in from the cold, into a wooden building already sagging with wear, where revolving doors now spin people into Scotia Place. Hurry was not a word appropriate to Mike's News Stand.

And it was more than that, more than a magazine store and smoke shop. It was the sporting centre of Edmonton. For sixty years, it was the ticket outlet for hockey, baseball, and football teams, and for the girl basketball players who first made Edmonton a city of champions.

TICKETS AT MIKE'S started in 1918. Billy Thompson, principal at Alex Taylor School, would be in at seven a.m. to open the box office. Mrs. Thompson took over when Billy left for school, but he'd be back at four. On cold mornings, when fans lined up in darkness in hope of buying tickets to see the Edmonton Athletic Club juniors play off against the St. Boniface Seals, Mike would be out on the sidewalk with free coffee.

He not only sold tickets for home games but provided scores of games away. Mike always wanted to know the score, being the greatest fan of all. Around 1920 he had a special telegraph wire run into the store. On game occasions, someone at a distant rink or field would send brief telegrams when something important happened. Mike would read them, for himself and his friends, as they printed out on the paper tape. When interested crowds grew too big for the store, he'd read them outside — through a megaphone, in the style of the man who introduced boxers at Madison Square Garden. Inside, meanwhile, teenagers hired for the occasion would be giving out scores to fans who phoned 22020 — perhaps the best-known number in Edmonton.

Then he and his pals Clyde Hook (of Hook Signs) and Colin Allen (of Colin Allen Electric) got into simulating play-by-play of distant hockey games. Fans on Jasper Avenue watched a glass screen, about ten feet square. From incoming telegrams Mike called the play through a megaphone, while behind the screen Clyde and Colin moved magnetic lights to illustrate the action. When the hated foes were on the attack, fans watched a red puck move towards the Eskimos' end of the ice. When the Eskimos attacked, a green puck would move. Certain players had unique styles well suited to the medium. Bullet Joe Simpson was also known as Corkscrew Joe for his twisting manner of rushing. When Joe was on the move, his progress was shown in a series of S-turns.

On the night of a big playoff game, crowds spread across Jasper to watch the moving lights and listen to Mike's play-by-play. Hockey announcers have their signatures: Foster Hewitt — "He shoots! He scores!"; Danny Gallivan — "A cannonading shot!"; Rod Phillips — "Oh-ooooooooooo!!". John Michaels' signature was "He's got the goalkeeper at his moicy!".

Hockey fans blocked traffic on hectic nights in 1923 when our Eskimos were in Vancouver playing the Ottawa Senators for the Stanley Cup. Firetrucks detoured to get to fires. Streetcars, unable to detour, had to stop and motormen joined the crowd.

Time and again they watched the green puck move towards the Ottawa goal and heard Mike call out, "Keats has got the goalkeeper at his moicy!" But too often Mike had to call, "Benedict saves!" Clint Benedict guarded the Senators' net, and he saved so often that our heroes came home without the Stanley Cup.

Mike's was not so much a place as an ambiance — the ultimate people-spot in a city that didn't count one hundred thousand people until the 1940s. It was an atmosphere — created by Mike himself and by the Three Musketeers, Bob, Bert, and Bill. Bob Wright was out at the back running Provincial News, the wholesale end of the business. He'd started with Mike in 1912, helping at the outdoor stand. Bert Millar, the store manager, came in 1920. Bill Brazil came in 1922, and all were there nearly fifty years, holding a bastion of permanence in a world built on sand.

Those who came in to Mike's people-place never felt rushed or pressured — least of all to buy. Although there may be no free lunch, at Mike's there was a free read. People could stand as long as their arches would support them reading magazines and papers, and were never bothered as long as they put their reading back where they found it. Some took flagrant advantage — for example, a university professor noted as much for his thrift as for his mastery of the English language — but Mike and the Musketeers were merely amused. Only a methodical freeloader would meet resistance — like the hotel janitor who went off shift at 10:30 p.m. and came in and stood reading *Argosy* till closing time. One night Bert Millar spotted "the method." The janitor would mark the place in his story by turning down a corner of the page and putting the magazine back in a certain position in the stack. Bert stayed after closing, chuckling to himself, and turning down different pages in all copies of *Argosy* in the stack. When Mike heard about it, he laughed out of control in the hearty rasp he'd brought from the sidewalks of New York, so hard that people enjoying a free read wondered what was going on in Mike's office.

There was usually something going on in Mike's office, a cluttered cubicle halfway down the store that featured a large smiling photograph of the Prince of Wales, snapped informally when the Prince came to Edmonton in 1919 and met Mike among others. With business in the sure hands of the Three Musketeers, Mike's office could be a hatchery for schemes enhancing the quality of community life. Like the veterans' Christmas dinner.

As the soldiers came home from the first war, Mike could see that many hadn't really come home to anything. With Christmas approaching in 1920, he was disturbed knowing these men would be eating Christmas dinner, if any, alone. So he put on the first of his dinners for them. Twenty-five came to the first. Some years there were ten times that many, and the tradition continues, supported by Mike's will.

The Newsboys Band flourished in the post-war era, taxing Mike's capacity for raising money and spending his own. They got so good that he sent them to Buffalo to play for a Shriners convention. In 1924, he sent them to England to play at the Wembley Exhibition. They were away for two months and en route home performed at the CNE in Toronto. In 1926, the band of the Coldstream Guards appeared at the Edmonton Exhibition and played in a massed band with Mike's Newsboys — the first time that Olympian British organization ever did such a thing. Some fine musicians came up though the band and not one Newsboy was ever judged by the courts to be a juvenile delinquent. Mike was proud of that.

In 1928, free-readers wondered why Moe Liebermann the lawyer and Harry Friedman the furniture man were spending so much time in Mike's office. Bowling was the subject. Travelling south of the border, Mike had noted the popularity of five-pin bowling, which made the ancient sport of Sir Frances Drake available to almost anyone. The result was the Recreation Bowling Academy — Mike liked the sound of *academy* — a two-storey people-place on 101 Street just across from Alberta College. For twenty-five years, "the Rec" was a warm spot in the city's heart and, like most of Mike's projects, breathed spin-off benefits for people who could use them — teenage pinboys who reset pins after each echoing crash, and old men who sat by the wall talking and called "Foul!" when a bowler's shoe slid over the line.

In 1931, Mike fulfilled a civic obligation with a neon sign, part of a campaign among business to brighten up Jasper Avenue. Jock McNeil the taximan raised $2,000 to string Christmas lights on the trolley poles. Gainer's put up a neon clock with a dancing pig on Jasper Avenue where it bends at 99 Street. The gas company raised a neon goddess high over Jasper, dispensing benefits of Alberta's natural resources. Mike's contribution was the man with the fedora, face buried in the *Toronto Star Weekly*, one leg swinging.

There was another sign associated with Mike's, a printed sign which appeared in the window once a week, usually Tuesday or Wednesday: OLD COUNTRY MAIL NOW IN. Mike had extended the principle of "Get your home-town paper!" to former residents of the British Isles, and brought in papers and magazines on an informal commitment to buy them. Kids sent to pick up the *Yorkshire Post* or *Liverpool Echo* were at the end of an exercise in speed — Liverpool to Montreal on CPR ships, Montreal to Edmonton on CPR express trains, all in ten days.

Of course, ideas about speed were being redefined by the airplane, and Edmonton was in the thick of that. Customers picking up their home-town papers at Mike's could read all about Edmonton on the front page of the *Chicago Tribune* or *St. Louis Post-Dispatch*, all about Wiley Post and Harold Getty and Jimmy Mattern landing here on round-the-world races against time, and all about the aerial hunt for the Mad Trapper.

Post and Co. were international celebrities. Our bush pilots were local heroes unique to Edmonton, pointed out on the street like star athletes. Free-readers in Mike's were bound to note the number of pilots who frequented Mike's crowded office. He was a fan of bush flying as the way to develop the north, which he pronounced to rhyme with sport. He became a fan in 1928 on a trip to Fort Simpson with his buddy Wop May, such a fan that he and Wop and Cy Becker and kindred spirits founded Commercial Airways, which eventually had six aircraft — operating on skis in winter and floats in summer. In 1929, when Gilbert Labine flew out of the north with the first uranium discovered at Great Bear Lake, he went straight to Mike's house for breakfast. In 1935, Mike was with fabled Joe Ayrington when he found pitchblende on Lake Athabasca and set off Uranium City.

On another northern adventure, Mike saved the life of bush pilot Archie McMullen. Archie was struck by a propellor and knocked unconscious into the Mackenzie River. Mike dove in to the rescue, and Archie was able to continue a career that took him to Canada's Aviation Hall of Fame.

In 1935, Mike was in with Charlie Garnett and Jay Jacox and the bunch who founded the Chamber of Mines, to promote the north's and Edmonton's just claim to be the gateway. Mike's enthusiasm could be a mixed blessing, as pilot Maurice Burbidge discovered. One winter day, Maurice was in his cockpit at the municipal airport, single engine running, overloaded plane rocking on its skis, thinking that with luck he'd just hurdle a distant fence. His calculated musings were shattered by a commotion and thumping behind. It was Mike — tossing in bales of magazines "for my friends down nort." No use arguing with Mike. Against all reason, the plane pulled its extra load off the snow and climbed towards the Arctic sky.

The second world war brought thousands of Americans to Edmonton, confirming the aviation community's contention that this was a world crossroads. Americans — 25,000 of them — came to build a highway and telephone line to Alaska, run an oil pipeline from Norman Wells to Whitehorse, and fly fighter planes and bombers to Russia. Mike had a special role in this explosion of activity. He was the city's unofficial envoy to the American zone commander. Mike and General Dale Gaffney were instant buddies, and the General presented him with another picture for his office — to go with the Prince of Wales. It showed the first four-engine plane over Edmonton, a C-54 military transport. The Macdonald Hotel stood properly in the foreground, but back among the low rises on Jasper Avenue the knowledgeable could identify Mike's News Stand.

When the war was over, Edmonton boomed on oil. Mike boomed too, enjoying the resurgence of optimism he'd met when he stepped off the train in 1912. Edmonton's once-and-future pride, the football Eskimos, was revived in 1949 with Mike front and centre. A giant pep rally at a drive-in theatre marked the resurrection. Mike was master of ceremonies and insisted that the coach be called "Anus Stukus." In 1951, another booster tradition — exhibition parades — was revived, with Mike as parade marshal. He announced, "It will be a brilliant display of colour and novelty and interest" — and lined up 133 entries, taking 90 minutes to pass. By this time, journalists from far-off Toronto, New York, and London were arriving to look down their noses at the Alberta oil boom. All wound up at the news stand to ask Mike to account for the prosperity. His answer was a few words from the realm of baseball, another of his enthusiasms: "It all dropped in our mitt!"

Mike's health was starting to let him down. A dragging bronchial problem forced him to spend winters away from the cold, but even in Florida he kept an eye open for things to enhance the quality of life in Edmonton. He played shuffleboard there and enjoyed it so much he sent four hundred dollars to provide a board for "them old guys at Government House" — then a rest home for disabled ex-soldiers, many of whom had been guests at Mike's Christmas dinners.

In 1963, Edmonton bade a reluctant farewell to John Michaels, but with the momentum he'd created, the Three Musketeers carried on the news stand through the '70s — a safe harbour for bewildered exiles returning to a town that seemed all out of shape, a spot secure and familiar among jarring high-rises. And time stood still in Mike's office, where his pictures stayed on the walls — the Prince of Wales and the first four-engine plane over the city.

But time was moving outside, relentless. Eventually the building went, with a blockful of others, for a high-rise called Scotia Place. The main entrance is on Jasper, where Mike's was, and where Edmonton was at.

Afterword

Edmonton has grown since I was added to the population in 1923. There were sixty thousand of us then. The city has grown upwards and outwards. The title of busiest intersection, claimed so long by First and Jasper, is held by the junction of Calgary Trail and the Whitemud Freeway. But through the growth, Edmonton has maintained a constant character, an unvarying civic personality.

This character was defined as early as May 24, 1906, when Grandfather Gorman discovered Edmonton on a trip to Ireland. Pressure of business in Chicago had undermined Sam's robust health to the point where his doctors recommended a long trip. Having yearned to see the green isle of his fathers, he booked a boat to Ireland; stopping in Ottawa to visit a brother, he was introduced to literature extolling the latest land of opportunity, the new province of Alberta. So he altered course for Edmonton. Arriving at the Canadian Northern Railway station (on 101 Street at 104 Avenue) near the end of the brief May night, he walked down to the top of McDougall Hill, gazed out on the river valley, and announced, "By God, we're going to build a city here."

Note that Sam hit on the word *we*. Only a few minutes in Edmonton and he had identified it as a city of champions — not in the sense of "one who wins first prize, especially in sports" but in the light of "one who supports a cause or another person." Before daylight reached down to the river flowing in the dark valley, he recognized Edmonton as a city of participants, a city in which, a century later, people would turn out in droves to make a success of the biggest Fringe Theatre Festival in North America; host the World Championships in Athletics; create aviation, telephone, and railroad museums in the face of official indifference; maintain standards of the Richard Eaton Singers; save CKUA; and, with the help of thirty-seven owners, participate in a strategy to keep Edmonton in the National Hockey League.

In Chicago, my mother Helen and six siblings got the surprising news that they were going to leave the second-largest city of the United States to build a new one in Canada. Arriving in Edmonton, gazing down on Jasper Avenue from a balcony of the Alberta Hotel, watching and listening to teamsters struggle with wagons in the mud, they could see that the city needed considerable building.

The population was arguably seven thousand — boosters would argue more, federal census officials less — but soon five incontrovertible residents were added. The Cashmans arrived from Orillia, Ontario, including my father, Walcott.

The family's path to Edmonton had been blazed by Great Uncle Dan Cashman during the Yukon Gold Rush. Great Uncle Dan was one of the 1500 who set out from Edmonton and one of the 800 who turned back and went through Skagway. But in passing, Dan obviously staked Edmonton's claim to Klondike Days. Family and friends in Ontario were left the forwarding address *Dan Cashman, Dawson City, Yukon Territory, Edmonton.*

Jack, my grandfather, was drawn by a softer lure. Running a men's clothing store in Orillia, he worked to one of the best-laid plans. He would work to age fifty, then enjoy total leisure in Canada's new west. But a few months convinced him that leisure, like any good thing, can be got too much of, and he began a second career of twenty years as business manager of the Federal Penitentiary on east Jasper Avenue — from which the prison farm extended north through the sites of Clarke and Commonwealth stadiums.

Meanwhile, Sam Gorman's entrepreneurial energies were at work. If we were to build a city, we would obviously need building supplies —

by the ton. Sam had never been in the business before, but he saw his duty. In the year 2002, a survey of G-8 countries identified Edmonton as the best place in the world to start a business — just what Sam and his pals told each other in 1906. They were boosters and made no secret of it. Academics may look down on boosterism as tasteless and bourgeois, but boosterism was a historic force with the power to raise cities. Sam's enthusiasm was well placed. The corporate name Gorman's Limited was around till merged out of existence not long ago, and a project still standing is the bridge over Groat Ravine on 102 Avenue.

In the 1930s, when rustic Groat Ravine was a favourite Sunday walk, Edmonton was a wonderful place to grow up. The city was safe, to begin. Just how safe could be observed where Groat Ravine came down to the river. The Edmonton Canoe Club stored its craft on racks in a shed with a roof and no walls, and never thought about vandals.

I grew up with memories of my father, a mining engineer who died at forty having never recovered from wounds of World War One. My brothers and I understood his niche in the history of warfare. The Military Medal we treasured had been awarded for courage on September 15, 1916, the date on which the tank first entered combat. In darkness before that dawn, Dad had led three into position.

Our mother had to take on the Depression as a single parent and returned to teaching, an earlier career interrupted briefly when she joined the first strike in the Catholic school system. This unique exercise in social activism occurred in 1919 when young lady teachers who lived at home left classrooms to help gain a living wage for male colleagues with families to support. Mother also resumed writing, with feature articles by Helen Gorman Cashman appearing in the *Journal*, including a series on our Chinese community. For this work she obtained — for twelve dollars — a second-hand Underwood typewriter. That thirty pounds of 1924 communications technology has remained in the family, and in service. All my writing has rolled from it, including these stories.

Edmonton was accepting the Great Depression with dignity, and though there were many poor people, there was little poverty — that insidious repeating cycle of hopelessness. Edmonton, the city of participants, was in full operation. The unique community leagues (begun in

Jasper Place in 1920) were improving the quality of life. At any moment Mrs. Carmichael, the dentist's wife, would be marshalling the musical, dramatic, and terpsichorean resources of the city to achieve four days of the Desert Song at the Empire Theatre. Weeks before natural ice made skating possible at the Glenora Club, members were working up routines for the highlight of the winter, the week-long Glenora Carnival at the Arena.

A lively Jewish community was a bonus. Half the parents were European; the kids were born in Edmonton in the 1920s — with names like Harry Ornest, Arthur Hiller, Joe Schocter, and Mel Hurtig.

Strange but true, in among the champion participants were champions in the sense of "one who wins first place, especially in sports." While other places doubtless had girls' basketball teams composed of graduates of one high school, the Grads of McDougall Commercial High were the best in the world — and proved it four times at the Olympic Games. Off the court, the world beaters were just neighbours. People could sit beside them on the streetcars, and with a mere seven carlines linking the entire city, opportunity knocked often. Outsiders looked at Edmonton and wondered why.

Then there were the bush pilots. Famous aviators ranked with star athletes. But while Charles Lindbergh was a distant mythic figure to all the world, stars like Punch Dickins, Wop May, and Grant McConachie, all local boys from well-known families, could be seen close up and in person going about the ordinary business of daily living. Outsiders looked at their achievements and wondered why. Geography certainly offered opportunity but they couldn't have made Edmonton Gateway to the North if the business community hadn't been committed participants.

Through family stories I was becoming aware of an earlier time. My uncle, P.R. Gaboury, told about being in the real estate boom which created a city with the area of Chicago (and a fraction of the population) before collapsing in 1914. Uncle George Gorman made the first commercial airplane flight in Alberta — in an open biplane — transporting June 10, 1919 editions of the *Edmonton Journal* to the Wetaskiwin fairground. Grampa Cashman was still with us. He had brought with him from Orillia the humorous insight of fellow townsman and customer Stephen Leacock, and told about the penitentiary and young prisoners he had befriended. Convicts had their heads shaved, and when they went out the gates, they were branded until their hair grew back. The Cashman household became a sort of halfway house for young men deserving a second chance. Stories flew when old friends dropped in, like Cleophas Turgeon, who had been the first town policeman. When there was a death in the French community, Mr. Turgeon would dress for the funeral in his best black suit and then go visiting. Frank Oliver and Matt McCauley and Carney the Blacksmith came alive again. It was interesting, but I didn't think of it as history. Conventional wisdom implied that only England had a history. Canada had a past of sorts. The west was too new for a past.

By the 1950s, this view was changing. I was in radio at CJCA incorporating the yarns into a long-running series called *The Edmonton Story* — and covering the current scene as a news reporter. News was mostly upbeat. The population was passing two hundred thousand. Oil was being discovered on all horizons. New people were coming in. Young people who had gone away to find work were coming back. And Edmonton was again producing champions in the realm of "one who wins first prize, especially in sports." The Flyers, Mercurys, and Eskimos were champions. The Grey Cup was on permanent display in the Macdonald Hotel, and the revival of football was an exercise in participation by the business community.

It was at this time that Edmonton began to annoy outside writers. First up was a man from New York, sent by *Time* magazine. Doubtless expecting a Texas-style wildcatter's atmosphere, he dismissed Edmonton as "the dullest boom town on earth."

All who came seemed baffled and frustrated by the civic character that Grandfather Gorman identified in 1906. They wondered why these things should be happening in Edmonton and why citizens should feel good about them. The most baffled and most annoyed was Canadian icon Bruce Hutchison, who passed this way writing a book called *Canada, Tomorrow's Giant*.

He was here for twelve hours, many of them sleeping at the King Edward Hotel, but experienced enough to be able to inform his readers that "there is no town in Canada so pleasantly egocentric, so childishly happy about everything as Edmonton. There is no town so well aware of its own perfections. Edmonton is the self-worshipping Narcissus of the nation."

The poor fellow didn't understand. Those who have come after don't understand. That is their misfortune. In the immortal words of the man at the back of the hall: "Three cheers for Edmonton."